CW01468350

Men.

WTF?

Copyright © 2024 by The Ultimate Breakup Coach (TUBC)

All rights reserved.

No portion of this book may be reproduced in any form without written permission from the publisher or author, except as permitted by U.K. copyright law.

This publication is designed to provide accurate and authoritative information regarding the subject matter covered. It is sold with the understanding that neither the author nor the publisher is engaged in rendering legal, investment, accounting, or other professional services. While the publisher and author have used their best efforts in preparing this book, they make no representations or warranties concerning the accuracy or completeness of the contents of this book and specifically disclaim any implied warranties of merchantability or fitness for a particular purpose. No warranty may be created or extended by sales representatives or written sales materials. The advice and strategies contained herein may not be suitable for your situation. You should consult with a professional when appropriate. Neither the publisher nor the author shall be liable for any loss of profit or any other commercial damages, including but not limited to special, incidental, consequential, personal, or other damages.

First Edition: 2024

Dedication

This book is dedicated to my Lee-Lee. Without your unwavering support, none of this would not have been possible. Oh, and it's also dedicated to Tom Hardy. Now that I know how to attract and keep my Mr. Right, I'm coming to get you!

Contents

Introduction

*H*ave you found yourself dating the same type of guy repeatedly? Have you ever noticed that different guys seem to bring up similar issues? It's almost like being stuck in a washing machine, rinsing, and repeating the same problems with different partners. My darling, if you believe improving your relationships means hoping your partner will change, it's like moving to a new house to avoid paying bills. Eventually, you'll have a new postie who delivers the same letters!

Oh, I am getting ahead of myself … Allow me to myself. My name is Kel, and I am a professional Breakup Coach. Every day, I have the privilege of helping others navigate the gut-wrenching aftermath of heartbreak. My main aim is to help them rebuild their self-esteem and encourage them to move forward and flourish after a difficult breakup. I've had the honour of working with people from all walks of life in all different situations, guiding them through their healing journey and empowering them to heal from their breakup. Let me tell you, there's no greater feeling than knowing I played a role in helping them get to that point. It fills me with so much gratitude to positively impact their lives during such a challenging time.

As a breakup coach, I have witnessed countless relationship dramas. From failed attractions and messy relationships to flirting mishaps, cheating scandals, and divorces, no topic is off-limits in my coaching sessions! Rest assured; I tackle every subject head-on. With over thirty years of personal experience and extensive research, I have gained valuable insights to make your eyes water.

It must be said that I've had my fair share of dating disasters and relationships. I know precisely what it is like to fall head over heels in love. But hey, I've also experienced my heart being shattered a few times (and yeah, I've broken a few hearts, too).

I've always been the go-to person for friends, family, and work colleagues who need relationship advice. My personal experiences, and more importantly, the mistakes I have made in the past, and realising what I should have done differently have empowered me to guide others through difficult times and offer clarity when things get confusing. That's why I decided to start my venture, Kels Coaching, to provide one-on-one breakup coaching, and in that, I found my true calling in life: helping people navigate the heart-wrenching pain of their breakup and heal. Nothing fills my heart more than seeing a client smile again and knowing I played some small part in their recovery.

So, following on from my life and coaching experience, I realised that I had, by default of my occupation, gained an insight into why relationships fail. So, I decided to write this book and share my knowledge, hoping it helps YOU! Although I coach both men and women, I could not write one book that helped all genders, so this book is for women who want to meet their dream man!

For so long, I had wondered why some relationships lasted whilst others failed miserably. Upon closer examination of the failed relationships, it appeared to me that most of these women had ended up with partners who were incompatible from the very start. They either ignored red flags at the beginning of the relationship or didn't prioritise (or even recognise) their individual needs and deal breakers. As a result, they jumped head-first into relationships, settling for someone who only partially fulfilled their needs. Unfortunately, these relationships were doomed to fail from the start.

I have seen numerous couples who stayed together for all the wrong reasons, such as financial stability or living arrangements, only to experience painful breakups later. My main aim is to delve into the reasons behind these unsuccessful relationships, provide insights to those who have faced similar challenges in their love lives, and increase your chances of recognising and attracting the right partner. With a current population of over 4 billion men, there is no excuse to settle for Mr. Wrong!

Ending with the wrong person or staying in a relationship for the wrong reasons can be a living, breathing nightmare. Often, we find ourselves in these situations because we subconsciously attract what we *believe* we deserve, which is a true reflection of our self-perception. How others treat us often reflects how we treat ourselves, and the people we are drawn to reflect how we, deep down inside, feel about ourselves.

Additionally, even when we meet a great guy, we often struggle to understand how men think, as their thought processes differ. It can be mind-boggling for us women to understand his thoughts and actions, and even harder to engage in meaningful conversations with men. However, by educating ourselves on these matters, we can make more informed decisions and hopefully find our happy ending and a relationship that lasts the test of time. After all, isn't that what we all want?

Many women I talk to get caught up in believing that dating is solely about finding their dreamy Prince Charming, their Mr. Right. They envision a guy who will swoop in, sweep them off their feet, and make all their dreams come true. They hope to be understood, adored, protected, cherished, and live happily ever after. However, here's the reality: obsessing over finding the "perfect" guy you've envisioned may cause you to overlook what truly matters; we think that it's ok that we do not have much in common, as he buys me flowers every week and walks the dog at night. I don't think anyone in history has broken up a happy relationship because they did not get flowers! In this book, we will go through the *real* dealbreakers in relationships.

You won't believe the number of people who think that finding "the one" will magically solve all their problems and make them happy. But instead of relying on others to fix everything for you, it's time to put the spotlight on self-improvement. Let me say it once more for good measure: the key lies in working on YOURSELF, not expecting miracles from a partner.

Instead of chasing a Cinderella fairy tale, this book aims to guide you in finding a relationship that genuinely brings you deep security, love, and happiness. It will teach you to look within yourself, identify your true desires in a relationship without limitations, boost your self-esteem, and trust your instincts. Doing so will ensure that when you meet your ideal man, your own Mr. Right, you will recognise him! Never again will you settle for a guy who won't be a good long-term match for you.

This, in turn, will increase your chances of not needing to employ me!

Prologue

The Mystery of Men & Dating

**"If you show a woman love, she will have love for a day…
But if you show a woman how to love herself, she will be loved for life."**

"So, why do we put ourselves through all this and still crave love?"

*L*ove has this funny way of causing us so much pain, yet we can't help but dream about it, right? We go through traumatic breakups, then we slowly heal our broken hearts, piece by little piece, and jump right back in for more, hoping to find our one true love, our "soul mate". Why do we keep risking more heartbreak? It's because nothing on Earth compares to the giddy feeling of being in love! If you could capture and bottle that indescribable feeling, you would undoubtedly be a billionaire!

Deep down, we all long for love and affection; it's human nature. If you listen to the greatest songs of all time, you'll notice that they overflow with lyrics about love – finding it, losing it, and dreaming about it. It's as if they speak directly to our hearts, reminding us that love truly makes the world go around.

Life is made for two, and being emotionally connected to someone brings numerous perks. It allows us to be our authentic selves without any reservations. We receive the support and reassurance we crave, feel heard and appreciated, and, most importantly, experience a sense of calmness and safety.

Having a strong romantic connection provides us with a feeling of stability. Having someone dependable by our side is reassuring, so we don't feel like we're navigating through life alone. Feeling safe and valued by those around us also boosts our self-esteem and keeps us in a positive mindset.

However, we do not live in a 'Once Upon a Time fairy-tale'; not all relationships are supportive and loving. Real life presents challenges, and relationships are bound to encounter difficulties, especially if you are with the wrong man. I have a hunch that you are aware of this reality already. The bottom line is that you deserve to be in a healthy, positive relationship where your needs are valued and respected.

There's a whole world of men out there, and just like there's a perfect-fitting lid for every saucepan, there's an ideal match for every woman. I'm here to help you spot your perfectly fitting lid!

Let me share a story about my buddy, Maddie. A while back, Maddie met this sweet guy who was arranging great dates and regularly called and texted her. But after they slept together ... she heard nothing. RADIO FREAKIN SILENCE! Her phone didn't ring the next day, and her text didn't ping either. And to make matters worse, he didn't contact her at all for the entire week.

This sudden silence made her feel worried, and her mind started racing with all sorts of questions:

Is he OK?
Did I say something wrong?
Has he fallen ill?
Has he gone off me?
Has his dog died?
Did he meet someone else?
Is he dead in a ditch?

After a few weeks of polar silence, Maddie couldn't handle it any longer and decided to give him a call. Unfortunately, he didn't answer, so she left him a message. But guess what? He didn't bother returning her call. To make matters worse, he had read her text message and ignored it anyway. Ugh! What the heck? Why wasn't he responding? Then, a few weeks later, her colleague spotted him on a dating site, so she knew he was perfectly fine. She never heard from him again, and to this day, she has no idea what went wrong.

Anyway, Maddie frantically searched the internet to find possible reasons why she got ghosted. She spent hours analysing it with her bestie, Sam, but eventually, she got over it and moved on. Just when she opened her heart to a new guy, guess what happened? He told her he was not looking for anything serious and suggested a friends-with-benefits arrangement. ARGHHHH!!

*"Welcome to the sh*t show of modern dating!"*

I cannot count the number of women I have encountered with my coaching who have had the same experience as Maddie. Let's be honest: Dealing with guys can sometimes be a bit frustrating for us ladies.

However, it can work out in your favour if you follow my two golden rules:

1. Learn to love yourself before expecting somebody to love you.

2. Learn to understand how men think (it's different from how we think, trust me) so that you have less conflict and more understanding in your relationships.

The truth is men and women are wired differently from the very core. It's not just about our choices; it goes much deeper than that. Our DNA and upbringing shape our unique characteristics right from the start.

"So, what gets in the way of finding that dream guy AND getting him to choose only me? How do I do this?"

As I have already said, men and women have unique ways of thinking. But instead of seeing these differences as a problem, we should embrace and appreciate them. Recognising this is key to better understanding and improving communication between us.

We may not always see things the same way, but gaining an understanding of how men think and behave can greatly improve your chances of forming a strong connection with your dream guy and reduce the likelihood of being ghosted.

I can practically hear you thinking, "Do we REALLY need an entire book to understand men?" Well, let's be honest: men can be confusing! I'm pretty sure you're not reading this book right now because everything is perfect in your love life. But guess what? I'm here to help you with just that!

This book is not about teaching you sneaky mind games or manipulative tactics. No, no, and thrice NO! I'm here to help you unlock the superpower of understanding how guys think and why. That way, you'll be able to communicate with them in a way that truly resonates. Pretty cool, right?

I'm sure you know that men and women have distinct ways of thinking and processing information. There's a reason for this, which I'll explain later in this book.

"But you're a woman; how can you possibly understand what goes on inside the minds of men?"

Well, let me share a little secret with you: I've dedicated many years to honing my skills in understanding people's thoughts and experiences, particularly in the realm of romance. It's almost like being an undercover secret agent in the dating world.Have you ever been in a situation where you expected a guy to respond to you the same way your female friends do? How has that worked out for you so far? It usually doesn't turn out well, does it? I've realised that if we want to get what we need from men, we must approach them with understanding. And the best way to do this is to understand THEM!

Don't worry; I would never encourage you to pretend to be someone you're not or change your personality or core beliefs. Instead, I aim to provide you with the knowledge and tools to navigate your relationships with men more effectively. No need to fake anything!

Through personal experience (the hard way), I've learned that playing games with men may seem tempting and yield short-term results. However, it only leads to confusion and heartache in the long run. The only guys who will appreciate the 'game' are the players, and we all want to avoid those types of guys, as we know where that leads, don't we?!

Trust me when I say that I've gone through my fair share of ups and downs to acquire this knowledge, and I am going to share it all with you right now!

Disclaimer: This book cannot possibly cover every individual and how he feels or thinks. I know everyone is different, and not everything I say may apply to every guy. Different men have their distinct traits and quirks (as we all know, right, ladies?).

So, grab a cup of tea (or a glass of vino), get comfortable, and remember, ladies – it's not about playing games. It's about communicating in a way that allows you to truly understand each other.

Let's dive in!

PART
ONE

Figuring Out What You Want

CHAPTER

1

"Be the kind of person you wish to meet."

*N*ow, here's a thought-provoking question that will make you pause... Would you date yourself? Think about that for a moment … REALLY think about it.

I don't just mean how attractive you are; I am also talking about traits like:

- Honesty.
- Standards.
- Confidence.
- Authenticity.
- Humour.
- Morals.
- Lifestyle.
- Goals.

We tend to attract people who are like us. You know what they say: we often become like the people we surround ourselves with. How often have you spent a lot of time with someone with a particular habit, and before you know it, you find yourself doing the same thing? I once worked with a lady who would say "Umm" before she answered a question, and I found myself doing the same thing after a while. Our friends and associates can truly shape who we are. Birds of a feather flock together!

So, it makes sense that if you are going to have a relationship, you will be exposed to the things your partner likes/does, etc., and so if you enjoy those things too, you have a far higher chance of the relationship thriving. Before attempting to understand men, you must first understand yourself – YOUR wants, needs, and what you bring to the table. For example:

- Looking to date someone spiritual? It's crucial that you both share a similar level of spirituality. This shared understanding can help in building a strong and meaningful relationship.

- You're looking for a guy who enjoys the same hobbies and way of life as you, right? The most effective strategy is to participate in those activities yourself right now. This way, you're not just increasing your chances of bumping into a man who might be your ideal match but is also having fun in the process.
- If you're hoping for him to be emotionally sound and maintain a positive outlook, it's crucial that you're in that space yourself.

It's all about walking the walk and setting the right example.

Before we delve deeper into things, do me a favour and grab a piece of paper. Write down a list of the EXACT kind of man you want to meet. Include his personality, drive, ambition, and anything else that is important to you. I want you to visualise him and imagine your life with him. Consider what he brings to the table and how your life together will look.

Let me ask you this: Are you fantasising about a dull, moody partner with no aspirations? No, you're not. And believe me, he isn't either.

"If you want a dream guy, you need to become a dream woman!" Before you sigh, let me tell you that this has NOTHING to do with beauty, weight, height, or how much money you have. It all comes down to how you behave, your attitude, and how you live your life!

Here's some straightforward advice: If you want to level up your dating game and avoid dead-end relationships or meaningless hook-ups, it's crucial to have a clear understanding of your absolute deal breakers, the things you could never accept or tolerate in a partner and refuse to settle for anything less. It's all too easy to get swept away by those super good-looking and charming men if you lose sight of what truly matters to you.

Be sure that your list does not include superficial needs. I've had a truly unexpected experience where someone I never thought would be my type pleasantly surprised me. On the flip side, someone who, on the outside, was 100% my type on paper … let me down!

Let me paint you a picture: A few summers ago, my best friend and I were soaking up the sun outside a bar, sipping cocktails. As we sat there, people-watching and enjoying the day, we started chatting with two guys at the next table. One was quite the looker – tall, fit and blessed with a silver tongue. Plus, he was in the army! The other chap was older, not as tall, and Didn't fit society's beauty standards. As we chatted into the afternoon, Mr Army Guy entertained us with his quick wit and humour, which only added to his charm. Then, out of nowhere, he spotted a man walking by who appeared to be homeless, and this man asked us for a spare change.

The army guy laughed at him and belittled him, leaving him feeling humiliated. The homeless man lowered his gaze in shame. But then, his mate stood tall and confronted the soldier, saying, "Don't talk to him like that." He pulled out a chair for the homeless man, offered a drink and food that was left over on the table, and showed genuine interest in his life story. This display of kindness and respect was so heart-warming that it completely won over my friend and I. Any spark we initially felt for the soldier quickly faded away. I often find myself reminiscing about that kind-hearted man – even now.

The man of your dreams is searching for a high-value, self-assured woman who recognises her own value. And guess what? That woman could be you! We all have unique quirks, likes, dislikes, and viewpoints that shape us into individuals. These high-value women often embody traits such as self-confidence, independence, integrity, and femininity. By cultivating these qualities within yourself, not only will you become irresistible, but you'll also attract the right person into your life.

"Why is it important for me to pick the right guy?"

Trust me, choosing the wrong person can seriously screw your life up and even have a lasting negative impact on your kids or future kids (should you choose to have any). If you're truly determined to snag your Mr. Right instead of Mr. Wrong, it's time to level up your dating skills. Don't depend on finding him to rescue you from a boring existence. This is the key: come closer … You must prioritise your OWN happiness and build a fulfilling life for yourself first. Once you've accomplished that, he'll quite possibly come and find you. Makes sense, doesn't it?

So, a few years ago, I had this neighbour who always talked about finding her perfect guy. She had this very specific idea of what her dream guy should be like. Now, just to clarify, she wasn't into working out, had no job, and hardly ever went out. But in her mind, amongst other things, her perfect guy would be super fit, love travelling, have amazing DIY skills, and be wealthy. It was almost as if she believed that finding this perfect guy would magically transform her into a completely different person, just to fit his lifestyle, and everything would be perfect.

Her theory was indeed interesting. However, she would have a much better chance of finding that kind of boyfriend if she put in the effort right now. Instead of fantasising about a man who would upgrade her life and change her for the better, she should focus on building her own fulfilling life that makes her happy. Then, if her ideal guy came along, he would just add to her already great life, and she would add to his.

Let's be honest: it would be unrealistic for me to expect to date someone who has a steady job, stays fit, and cooks fancy meals from scratch if I spend my days unemployed, watching Netflix, smoking, and only eating KFC. Let's face the reality: a significant gap between our values and lifestyles would exist. I'm not entirely confident about how well we would connect if I pursued a relationship with Mr. Right without first focusing on myself and being happy with myself and who I am.'

I wholeheartedly agree that pretending to be someone you are not is never the way to go. You should never need to change your looks, life, or personality just to attract a guy. Instead, I encourage you to think about your ideal guy and life and focus on creating that for yourself. It's about being true to yourself and attracting someone who loves and appreciates you for that.

So, on that note, I am adding some space here so you can jot down EXACTLY what your dream guy would be like. No holds barred; it's for your eyes only! …

My ideal man would be ...

The reason he would enhance my life is:

_____

_____

_____

_____

_____

_____

_____

_____

_____

_____

_____

_____

_____

_____

_____

_____

_____

So, now you have the list and know what you want, let's work out how to meet and keep this amazing guy!

CHAPTER

2

"There is no such thing as 'too fussy'".

*I*f I had the chance to go back in time and give advice to my teenage self, here's what I would say:

"Be extremely selective when choosing a partner or a father for your children."

I've said it before, and I'll say it again: selecting the right partner or husband is one of the most crucial decisions you'll make in your life. That's why making a wise decision in this matter is essential. Update your list above as you go along if more things come to mind.

When it comes to finding a partner and planning your life, it's crucial to be honest about your true desires. Take the time to understand what you truly want, as it will lead to a fulfilling relationship and the life you deserve. Release any limiting beliefs. For example, if you truly desire a religious, sporty, or family man, own it! Identify your deal-breakers non-negotiable) and what superficial needs (which can be negotiated) are. Start recognising what truly matters to you. It's time to stop holding yourself back and give yourself the freedom to chase your dreams and live life to the fullest!

- If you desire a man who can provide for you, embrace that desire.
- If you want a man to protect you fiercely, embrace that desire.
- If you want a chilled, laid-back man, embrace that desire.
- If you want a spiritual man, write it down.

If you're looking to explore your desires, I have a suggestion for you: journaling! It's incredibly easy to get started. All you need is a pen and paper. Simply begin jotting down whatever comes to your mind – thoughts, dreams, goals – anything! Trust me, it has been a game-changer for many of my coaching clients.

Once you've figured out what you want, it's crucial to set non-negotiable standards for yourself. These will be your personal guidelines, helping you stay focused and achieve your goals.

Here are some examples of standards:
- A guy who is compassionate and understanding.
- A guy who is serious about settling down and values family and marriage.
- A guy with integrity.
- A funny guy.
- A generous and loving guy.
- A guy who knows how to treat others with respect.
- A guy who is consistent and completely infatuated with you (no wishy-washy or unsure behaviour).
- A guy who makes you feel safe.
- No sex without commitment.

Those were just a few random examples I came up with to give you an idea. However, it's important to remember that YOU set your standards!

Let's write these lists down before we begin so that your idea is as clear as possible.

Write down your Non-Negotiable needs:

Now jot down your preferred needs (can be negotiated)

_____

_____

_____

_____

_____

_____

_____

_____

_____

_____

_____

_____

_____

_____

_____

_____

_____

_____

_____

_____

These needs are your own and dependent on what YOU want and what makes you feel good. So, go ahead and set them however you like! Don't worry about what society or others expect from you. Their opinions shouldn't control your desires. Instead, focus on what truly feels right and will bring you happiness. Trust yourself, listen to your inner truth, and do not be scared to ask for it. If you have more realisations as the book goes on, then come back and add to the lists.

"So, how do I figure out what kind of guy I want?2

Let's talk about the importance of creating a list of must-have qualities to find the perfect partner. Whether you're looking for someone to start a family with a great stepparent for your kids, or someone to travel the world with, it's important to get clear on what you're truly looking for. It's easy to think that physical attractiveness or great sex is the most important factor, but just like I mentioned earlier, with 'Army Guys ', muscles, good looks, and fancy cars don't necessarily reflect someone's ability to be an amazing partner or parent.

Instead, focus on what truly matters– kindness, empathy, humour, future plans, shared values, and life goals. In the grand scheme of things, it's the intangible qualities that make someone truly amazing when it comes to building a solid and loving relationship. You know, the qualities that go beyond looks or material possessions. These are the things that matter when you're building a life together and, perhaps, even considering raising a family.

Let's be honest: does his physical attractiveness REALLY matter if he can't meet your needs?

Consider this: Will his good looks and sexy eyes still be appealing when you're exhausted and overwhelmed with responsibilities? Moreover, if you prioritise his wealth, what's the point of money if he wastes it on luxury cars, drugs, other women, gambling, or alcohol instead of taking care of his family?

When making your list, it's crucial to aim for qualities that will have a lasting impact. Consider the long-term effects they will have on your life and your children's lives, whether they're already here or will come along in the future. Don't compromise your values out of insecurity or fear of being alone. It doesn't matter how attractive or wealthy someone may be; stay true to your values and don't settle for anything less. When it comes to how guys behave, it's important to assess if their actions align with your beliefs and desires.

"There aren't enough good men around. How will I ever meet anyone?"

I have many clients and friends who are convinced that they will never meet Mr. Right.

The issue with this mindset is that if you consistently believe that there aren't enough men who meet your criteria (which can occur if you're trapped in a negative mindset), chances are, you'll settle for less than what you truly deserve, repeatedly (sound familiar?).

You might worry that there are no good guys left out there, or perhaps you find yourself settling for just anyone who shows interest due to your lack of confidence. You will just be grateful for the attention. Maybe you think he has potential if you can change certain things about him, or maybe it just feels good to have someone interested in you. But please remember, the only person you can change is yourself!

I mean, I get it. Finding the perfect match can be a real challenge. You might worry that no good guys are left out there. You may worry that if you are too fussy, you will be single forever. We've all been there, trust me. But here's the thing: you should never settle for just anyone out of desperation or loneliness. You deserve someone who brings what you need to the table, truly appreciates your worth, and loves you for exactly who you are. Being with the wrong guy is far worse than being single; I promise you that!

There are numerous reasons why people end up with the wrong person, but it's often the fear of being alone that keeps them stuck in that relationship, even though they are not happy.

"But why would the dream guy I'd want to be with even choose to be with someone like me?"

If you tend to underestimate yourself, it could result from low self-esteem. This can make you more vulnerable to becoming overly attached to someone of the opposite sex who gives you attention. It's completely understandable, right? When you're feeling down about yourself, receiving attention from a guy can boost your ego. It feels amazing, and you may become addicted to that validation.

Ultimately, it boils down to how you perceive your worth. How do you see yourself? Can you recognise the same positive qualities that someone who pays attention to you sees? Most importantly, what compliments or actions specifically make you feel confident and attractive?

I've had numerous conversations with women whom I coach, who find themselves stuck in a cycle of seeking validation from men. But the truth is, they believed that being with *anyone* was better than being alone. However, deep down, they truly desired a genuinely satisfying and fulfilling relationship. That's why it's crucial to never settle for anything less than what you deserve!

"Why do I always attract toxic guys?"

The answer is simple: we attract all different types of people. However, when someone we find physically attractive gives us the attention we crave, some women ignore the glaring red flags and become blinded by their affection and good looks. They start to feel comfortable with the attachment, even if it's unhealthy because it's better than nothing (or so they think). They make excuses for his inappropriate behaviour. Some stay in these toxic relationships for months or years, while others stay for a lifetime.

Sometimes, people even get married due to societal expectations or the desire to have a family before their biological clock ticks away. The fear of being alone can drive some people to make insanely poor decisions. The more time you spend learning to value yourself and act on red flags, the fewer toxic people you will have in your life. This applies not only to romantic relationships but also to family and friends. If you can lose any fear you may have of 'being alone,' then you will never feel the need to get into – or stay in – a bad relationship. This, my darling, is a superpower!

So, let's talk about the red flags you need to look out for when you meet a new guy.

CHAPTER

3

"Red Flag Here, Red Flag There"

*B*efore we continue, I want to delve deeper into the topic of red flags, as it is so important. These warning signs are often overlooked or dismissed when we first meet someone; sometimes, they are not visible until much later in the relationship. By ignoring red flags, you disregard your boundaries and put your well-being at risk. Each time you choose to ignore these warning signs, you unintentionally allow others to continue their unacceptable behaviour. It's important to recognise and address these red flags so that you can prioritise your well-being & self-respect and establish healthier boundaries.

You chip away at your self-worth and undermine your self-respect whenever you ignore a red flag. It's crucial to be mindful of these warning signs for the sake of your personal growth and well-being. By acknowledging these red flags, you can empower yourself and nurture a stronger sense of self-love.

"Seeing the good in someone" can sometimes be used as an excuse to avoid confronting them about their negative behaviour. If you need to try to find the good in someone, it may indicate that you are simply making excuses for their actions. It is important not to overlook the toxic traits that can indicate potential future problems in a relationship. Let's explore a few of these warning signs in men.

He seems to be controlling.

Recognising controlling behaviour in men is crucial, as it could be a sign of a toxic relationship. This type of behaviour may indicate an unhealthy power dynamic. It can manifest as making decisions without considering your input or trying to control your actions. Spotting these signs early on is extremely important, as they can significantly impact your emotional and physical well-being. By identifying them, you can act and prioritise taking care of yourself.

He's unreliable, and you cannot trust him.

Doubts about your partner's trustworthiness are a major red flag in a relationship, and trust is crucial for a healthy and thriving partnership. It's a simple concept that must be reliable and dependable to build trust. When your partner consistently disappoints you or does not keep their promises, it can seriously damage the bond between you. This can lead to feelings of resentment and uncertainty, ultimately harming the relationship.

He seems to be manipulative.

If you start noticing his manipulative behaviour, that's a red flag. It means he's trying to control you, which is unacceptable. Manipulation often involves playing with your emotions or exploiting your vulnerabilities just to get what they want. They might even make you feel guilty or shame you to achieve their goals. Trust me, this kind of person can mess with your head and make you feel powerless in the relationship. And let's not forget how confusing it can be, too!

He's rude and doesn't care about other people's feelings.

If you're curious about someone's true character, pay attention to how they treat others. If your partner consistently disrespects you or other people, that's a red flag. It's even more concerning if they don't value your feelings and opinions or if they're rude to waitstaff or family members. These behaviours indicate a lack of respect, empathy, and consideration for others – qualities that can be challenging to deal with in a relationship.

He accepts no responsibility when he messes up.

In any relationship, both individuals must take ownership of their actions. This applies not only to relationships but also to life in general. When someone avoids taking responsibility, it may indicate a lack of maturity or willingness to be accountable. Meaningful conversations become challenging when your partner constantly shifts the blame or refuses to admit their mistakes. Essentially, without accountability, it becomes nearly impossible to have productive conversations. (This is something to be mindful of in yourself, too, as it is an easy trait to identify in others but hard to identify in yourself.)

H has mood swings.

Dealing with guys who have mood swings can be quite challenging. One moment, they're fine; the next, they're exploding with anger and irritability. It creates a stressful and unpredictable atmosphere that keeps you on your toes all the time.

He labels all his exes as "bonkers".

When a guy labels all his ex-partners as "bonkers," it's time to raise your eyebrows. It gives the impression that he believes every breakup he's had was solely due to his partners rather than acknowledging his own contribution to the issues. This shows a lack of self-awareness and an unwillingness to take responsibility for what went wrong in his past relationships. It also suggests an inability to learn from mistakes, which is likely to result in repeating those same mistakes in future relationships.

He seems jealous or possessive.

At first, you might mistake these actions as signs of affection, thinking that he likes you because he's jealous, right? WRONG! These actions can be red flags, indicating controlling tendencies. Jealousy brings about negative emotions, and possessiveness is a way of trying to control someone. Furthermore, if he feels threatened by others, it shows a lack of self-confidence.

He gaslights you.

Gaslighting is a significant and alarming red flag when it comes to a person's behaviour. It is crucial not to dismiss it lightly. Gaslighting involves manipulating someone to doubt their reality and distorting their memories. This form of manipulation can manifest in various ways, like minimising the victim's emotions or denying events that undeniably occurred. It is important to recognise that gaslighting is completely wrong and can have a profound impact on one's mental well-being.

He puts in too little effort.

It could be a warning sign if he isn't putting in much effort. It suggests that he may not be fully committed or willing to invest in the relationship. Men who show little motivation or hesitate to give their time and energy may be indicating that they aren't seeking a long-term relationship. This can lead to problems such as an uneven power dynamic, where one partner isn't receiving the care, they deserve.

He puts in too much effort.

On the flip side, let's not forget that putting in TOO MUCH effort (over the top) can raise some concerns for totally different reasons. This could suggest that he suffers from low confidence and lacks trust, or he has a lack of confidence and doesn't prioritise his own needs or boundaries. It might also imply that he is too clingy and reliant on you excessively, which can be quite overwhelming.

He's starting to get aggressive with you.

Being super aggressive can be a MASSIVE red flag when it comes to guys. It suggests that they might struggle with healthily managing their emotions. People who are prone to aggression can easily become agitated and may resort to threats or even physical violence to make their point. This type of behaviour creates an unsafe and toxic atmosphere, putting everyone at risk of serious harm.

He is selfish.

If a guy is selfish, it could indicate that he is solely focused on his own needs and disregards the feelings and needs of others. This self-centred behaviour can hurt the entire relationship, creating an unhealthy and imbalanced dynamic. If he prioritises his happiness above all else, it is likely that you won't feel valued or have your own needs fulfilled. In a healthy relationship, both individuals should genuinely care about each other's well-being and strive to make each other feel happy and secure.

He blames his childhood and past relationships for his mistakes.

I must be real here. Regardless of the challenges someone has faced in their childhood or the toxic relationships they've been in, it doesn't excuse them from behaving badly or mistreating others. When a man starts blaming his past for his current actions and refuses to take responsibility, it's a BIG warning sign. It shows that he isn't willing to change or admit his mistakes. Moreover, let's not forget how this can be a sneaky way of manipulating others by shifting the blame away from himself.

He doesn't listen to you.

If a guy isn't listening to you, it's not a good sign. It shows that he's not interested in what you're saying, which can make you feel down. Your opinions should always matter, and feeling ignored is never okay in any relationship. Moreover, if he's unwilling to see things from your perspective, it can lead to some heated arguments, too.

He doesn't seem to care about your personal space and boundaries.

It's 100% concerning when he doesn't respect your boundaries. It shows that he isn't considering your feelings and doesn't take your happiness seriously. People who don't respect boundaries are more likely to exploit others, which is even worse. When your limits and preferences are disregarded, it can make you feel unappreciated and insignificant. Just a reminder, this applies to situations where you've communicated your boundaries to the person involved, especially when it comes to protecting yourself from harm.

He 'love-bombs' you.

When it comes to guys, love bombing is a major red flag. It's a sneaky tactic used to manipulate and control people. The whole idea is to quickly gain your trust and admiration by showering you with compliments, gifts, and a lot of attention. It might stroke your ego and make you feel incredibly special, but don't fall for it – it's all just a show. Love bombing is often associated with narcissistic individuals who enjoy playing mind games. Sometimes, spotting manipulative behaviour isn't easy. If your gut feeling tells you that someone seems too good to be true or something doesn't quite add up, trust your instincts and stay sharp. (More on this later.)

He isn't concerned about your safety.

If a guy couldn't care less about your safety, that's a major red flag. It means he's not interested in keeping you safe or looking out for you. And let's face it, who wants to be in a relationship filled with fear and insecurity? Feeling safe is something that should never be compromised. So, if he can't even be bothered to check if you've arrived home safely, it's time to kick him to the curb and find someone who genuinely cares about your well-being. Those seemingly small acts of consideration can make a world of difference in creating a loving and secure environment.

He isn't honest with you.

Being honest is incredibly important in any relationship. If your partner isn't genuine with you, that's a significant warning sign. Trust and dependability are essential for a healthy partnership. Without trust, the entire relationship is likely to fall apart. When someone betrays your trust in a major way, it's extremely difficult to rebuild that connection—and it's understandable. If they have let you down in the past, it's completely normal to question whether they will do it again.

His actions and words do not align.

When it comes to reliability and trustworthiness, it's crucial to follow through on your actions. If a guy can't back up his words with actions, or he promises to take you somewhere or give you something and then forgets about it or does not follow through, it's a warning sign. It can make you question his trustworthiness and create insecurity in the relationship. After all, who wants to be with someone they can't rely on, right? It might also indicate laziness or a lack of commitment, which will likely worsen over time.

"But why is it so important to watch out for red flags?"

At the end of the day, paying attention to warning signs like these is crucial. This helps identify unhealthy traits that could potentially lead to a toxic relationship. Being aware and attentive to red flags can save you from potential heartache in the future. Always trust your gut if you notice any concerning behaviour. It's crucial to pay attention to your instincts. How you handle red flags depends on their seriousness and what you find acceptable based on your values and boundaries, which we established in Chapter 2.

When you're feeling doubtful about something in your relationship, it's important to talk about it straight away in a way that does not sound accusatory. By being open and honest, you give your other half the chance to understand where you're coming from and maybe even switch up their behaviour. Communication is key for creating a solid and caring bond—there's every chance they might not have realised how much their actions were getting to you.

If you notice any red flags, feeling concerned is perfectly normal. But don't panic just yet! While they may indicate potential issues, it doesn't necessarily mean the deal is doomed. Take a moment to relax and assess the situation. Whether it is a deal breaker or not depends on the people involved and the specific circumstances. We all have different boundaries and things we're willing to overlook in a relationship.

Certain things should make you seriously reconsider a relationship. If he is making you feel unsafe, that's a big red flag, and it's best to cut ties immediately. Then, there are those other warning signs that require some monitoring. These could go either way—they might be resolved through communication and effort or escalate into something more frequent or serious.

Believe me when I say that nothing good comes from ignoring red flags.

I get that when you have strong feelings for someone, it can be tough to acknowledge any warning signs that arise. It may feel easier to ignore them, especially when you've waited so long to feel a connection with someone. However, it's crucial to remember that ignoring those red flags will only bring you more pain in the future. It's better to confront them directly and avoid unnecessary heartbreak later. Trust your gut feeling if you're unsure whether something is a red flag. Your instincts are there for a reason! If it made you angry, scared, or disappointed, your emotions are trying to tell you that something is off. Stay vigilant and watch out for any warning signs. This way, you can improve your chances of finding a safe, healthy, and truly fulfilling relationship.

"Love-Bombing"

This is a 'sneaky' red flag that can make you feel like you have met 'the one' at the start of a relationship. It's a scary trait because it is disguised as extreme interest, and you do not see it coming. It does not seem like an issue at the beginning because you might have been flattered by the attention initially.

You can recognise genuine romantic interest when someone shows a strong connection to you and eagerly looks forward to getting to know you better. They genuinely enjoy spending a lot of time with you and take the initiative to plan dates and hangouts. They remember what you tell them, suggest activities that align with your interests, and ask questions to deepen their understanding of you. It all feels natural and normal.

Love bombing, however, is the darker side of dating and something to be cautious of, so I need to point this out to you. Many people have never even heard of love bombing, but it is a significant red flag in a new relationship. Initially, your partner may shower you with expressions of love after only a few days or weeks. They may even claim that you are their soul mate, the person they've been waiting for their whole life. They might even insist on introducing you to their family, emphasising how much they need you. They could talk about moving in together, getting engaged, offering gifts, and making grand gestures shortly after meeting them, and it may feel too soon.

However, this is often an attempt to rush intimacy, creating a false impression of a deeper connection that has yet to be fully established.

Examples of love-bombing include:

- Receiving a constant stream of compliments that makes you feel flattered yet uncomfortable at the same time. These compliments may focus on your physical appearance, sometimes crossing into inappropriate or sexual territory. However, it's important to recognise that they often lack depth and substance, which can give you a false sense of uniqueness and significance.
- Making promises too early, like saying "I will never leave you" or "We will last forever," or rushing things and demanding commitment within a few weeks are things to be leery of. It's important to take the time to get to know someone and establish a strong foundation before making these commitments.
- When someone tells you shortly after meeting that you are "soul mates" or "meant to be," it's important to approach such sentiments with a touch of scepticism. While they may make you feel special and loved, it's crucial to remember that these declarations may not necessarily be true at such an early stage.
- Saying, "I love you" very quickly, within days or weeks (BIG red flags), as deep bonds tend to take a while to develop for most people and to love someone, you must know them. You cannot get to know a person in a few days/weeks,

- Excessive or constant communication and getting angry if you don't reply quickly enough.
- Disrespecting your boundaries and pressuring you into things, especially of a sexual nature, that you are not ready for. Moreover, they may resort to emotionally manipulating you, intentionally starting arguments over trivial matters, which can leave you feeling upset and dependent on them.
- Discussing future aspirations, such as vacations or starting a family together, talking about moving in together or getting married after a few weeks of being together (MASSIVE RED FLAG)

Believe it or not, some people may not even realise that they are guilty of love bombing. It's not always a calculated manipulation tactic. Sometimes, individuals simply crave the excitement and euphoria of being in love so much that they unintentionally engage in this behaviour. They might be desperate to find a partner and dislike being alone, which causes them to rush through important steps in forming a genuine connection with someone. These people need to also be approached with caution.

However, love bombing is often a manipulative tactic used by abusive individuals to make someone fall for them. The question arises: do they employ this strategy out of insecurity and desperation for love, or are they intentionally targeting someone to manipulate? In most cases, it is likely the former, although some abusers may also resort to love bombing.

CHAPTER
4

"Self-loathing vs Self-love"

*Y*ou've probably come across the saying that to find love, you need to start by loving yourself. This isn't just a cliché—it's a fundamental truth. Self-love is crucial because, without it, finding the kind of love you're looking for can be an uphill battle.

I have conversations with numerous women each week who hold the belief that finding their perfect partner will be the key to loving themselves and achieving everlasting happiness. They have the notion that their ideal man will fill the void in their life and bring them the happiness they long for. They often express their feelings of loneliness and their belief that meeting an incredible man will completely transform their lives and bring them the happiness they seek.

When I hear this, it weighs heavy on my heart because I know for a fact that this is not the case at all.

"What do you mean?"

Well, telling yourself that someone else on this planet will be the sole source of your happiness is one of the biggest lies you can tell yourself. The cold, hard truth is that the key to true happiness lies within yourself.

Many women rely on external validation from a partner to determine their self-worth and boost their self-esteem, but this can be a very dangerous path to take. The problem lies in the fact that as quickly as someone else can make you feel amazing, they can just as easily turn off the tap and make you feel terrible. And then, what do you do? This is why it's imperative not to rely on someone else to make you feel happy or good about yourself.

"How can I determine if I have low self-esteem?"

Ahhh, well, you may have low self-esteem if you:
- Are extremely critical of yourself.
- Ignore or downplay your positive attributes.
- Believe you are inferior to others.
- Use negative descriptions when describing yourself.
- Use negative self-talk all the time.
- Never take credit for your own achievements; instead, put it down to luck or a fluke.
- Never believe or dismiss compliments about yourself.

"So, what causes low self-esteem?"

Numerous factors can greatly affect your self-esteem, oftentimes it stems from childhood experiences. It could be influenced by the way you were parented, your relationships with siblings, or even your interactions with teachers or peers at school.

Many individuals with low self-esteem have endured bullying regarding their appearance while growing up, and these negative experiences tend to linger and impact their self-perception. Additionally, past relationships or friendships can also contribute to low self-esteem, as individuals may internalise the criticisms or belittlement they have received.

Everyone's life experience in life is unique, and it would take more than this book to cover everything. However, it is important to reflect on your past and understand where your feelings of low self-worth come from. If this is how you are feeling, it's crucial to address it.

The good news is that you have the choice to be a woman with high self-esteem or a woman with low self-esteem. You can choose to explore the reasons behind your negative feelings about yourself and make the necessary changes. This decision has the potential to be one of the best you've ever made.

Women with high self-esteem are kind to themselves. They forgive themselves for the mistakes they make and learn from them. They engage in positive self-talk and trust themselves to make the right decisions because they approach themselves with love, trust, and respect. These women tend to succeed because even in the face of failure, they maintain self-belief. They pick themselves up and try again until they achieve success.

Everyone has an internal dialogue (self-talk). A woman with high self-respect firmly believes in herself and will not tolerate any form of shady or disrespectful treatment from anyone. She understands that we teach others how to treat us and sets clear boundaries accordingly. Disrespecting such a woman is incredibly difficult because she simply will not tolerate it.

On the flip side, women with low self-worth often engage in negative self-talk, belittle themselves, disregard their own abilities, and lack belief in themselves. Consequently, they may struggle to succeed as their self-talk convinces them that they are incapable of accomplishing things. This negative mindset often becomes a self-fulfilling prophecy.

A woman with low self-worth is more susceptible to finding herself in abusive and toxic relationships. Deep down, she believes that is all she deserves. She may choose to stay with the wrong man because she feels fortunate to have him, even though she knows he isn't the right fit for her. Despite not truly loving him, she opts to remain in the relationship because it feels preferable to being lonely and single, which further reinforces the negative self-image she has developed.

Listen, life is short, and none of us are getting out of this alive. Even if we live to be 120 years old, it will still pass by in a flash. That's why it's crucial to prioritise living a happy and fulfilling life. If you find yourself caught in a cycle of self-hate, low self-esteem, and low self-respect, you're setting yourself up for extreme misery. However, it doesn't have to be this way.

When you have low self-esteem, you tend to rely on others to boost your confidence and validate your worth. However, with high self-esteem, you come from a place of power and do not depend on others to affirm your value. You no longer emit an energy of desperation and instead attract healthy, decent people into your life. You have the strength to reject any form of toxic behaviour, as you have a strong sense of self-worth.

For this reason, it is important to cultivate self-love and learn to respect and admire yourself. However, it's also important to note that this should not be mistaken for arrogance or self-centeredness, as, let's be honest, those traits are not attractive.

"But how can I learn to love myself?"

Ahh, well, learning to love yourself starts with your self-talk. How you talk to yourself is incredibly important because, my darling, YOU are listening!

Loving and respecting yourself is the first step towards receiving love and respect from others. Let's face it: this can be a real challenge for many of us. However, it's crucial to focus on loving the person you see in the mirror. Take some time to truly understand yourself – your strengths, weaknesses, what you admire about yourself, and areas where you'd like to grow.

Let's go back to journaling. To get this done, find a peaceful spot where you can have a real heart-to-heart with yourself. Grab a notepad and begin by jotting down all the fantastic qualities that make you awesome. Then, take a moment to list out any self-doubts or reasons you might think you're not deserving of love. Once your 'not deserving of love' list is ready, go through it without being too hard on yourself. Check if there's any concrete proof for those beliefs in the real world – chances are, it's just a feeling making you feel unworthy rather than actual evidence.

It's crazy how our brains can play tricks on us when we're dealing with low confidence, making us think we're not good enough. Sometimes, we start blaming ourselves for our anxiety, thinking that there's something wrong with us. But here's the thing: you're not flawed or broken. You just need some healing.

So, next time those unworthy feelings creep in, challenge your thoughts. Remind yourself that you are deserving of respect and love. And if you want to attract more positive people into your life, make sure to treat others with the same respect and love that you seek from them. It's all about giving back what you want to receive!

If you want to make some improvements in your life, start by taking small, doable steps towards the things you can change and really want. As for the stuff you can't change, it's important to embrace your imperfections and accept that nobody's perfect. Remember, it's okay to have flaws! Sometimes, what you see as a flaw could be the very thing that makes you special and attracts people to you. Also, don't hesitate to expect more from the people around you. Making sure you set boundaries and stand your ground is super important if you want to attract good vibes into your life.

When you catch yourself putting yourself down, it's important to change that negative self-talk and instead give yourself compliments. Take a moment to look at yourself in the mirror and appreciate even the things you may not like. Find a way to learn to like and even (dare I say it) love those aspects because they make you unique. Remember, there is only one you in this world, and you are truly amazing – even your imperfections rock!!

"But how do I start this?"

Well, starting from this minute onwards, I encourage you to speak to yourself with the same love and kindness that you would use when talking to your most cherished loved ones, whether it's your family, best friends, or children. You would never speak about them the way you sometimes do about yourself, I'm sure.

If you have ever been bullied or treated poorly in the past, then it's important to take a step back. Reflect on the individuals who have done this to you and truly see who they are. It's crucial to forgive them and yet realise that they were wrong. I suggest forgiving them because holding onto anger is like drinking poison and expecting the other person to die.

You'll find that when people put you down and make you feel bad about yourself, it's usually because, deep down, they feel bad about themselves. They try to project their negativity onto others to feel better about themselves. I've never understood this concept, but it happens. However, you have a choice. You can either let these people get into your head and make you feel bad, or you can pick yourself up, dust yourself off, and not let them ruin the rest of your life.

So, on that note, it is essential to put an end to self-deprecating behaviour right now. Always remember that you have full control over this decision, and it will never benefit you to continue to self-loath. It's time to recognise your own greatness and start behaving accordingly.

Think about it this way: the chances of your birth are incalculable. Out of all the billions of people in this world, what were the odds of your parents meeting and creating you in that moment? You are a walking, talking miracle. So, why waste your precious time on this earth by harbouring self-hate, putting yourself down, and tolerating unhappy relationships? I am here to help you turn things around and find the love you truly deserve. Remember, it all starts with loving yourself.

Now, let's discuss how you can raise your standards and find a great guy, thus increasing your chances of finding lasting love...

CHAPTER 5

"Chase or be chased?"

*A*lright, bear with me because I'm about to dive deep…

As complex human beings, we often use various methods to find a partner. We may follow our hearts, seek help from friends, try online dating, go on blind dates, or even take part in singles nights and speed dating. However, you may have noticed that nature has its unique way of selecting mates in the animal kingdom. In many animal species, females can decide whether to accept or decline males' advances and courtship behaviours.

You might be thinking, "What does this have to do with me? Don't compare me to a goat!" But hang on, let me explain.

You know that pattern you see in nature? Well, turns out it's common in the world of human dating too. People have been doing it for centuries! But here's the thing: with all this internet and movie stuff, we've started to think we're way smarter than those animals. And in the process, we've kind of forgotten the basics.

Even in today's modern world, some old-school traditions are still in fashion. One such example is the act of asking for permission to marry. Yes, it's still a thing! Men still ask their lady's father for his blessing to marry his daughter, and women still have the final say in whether they accept or reject the proposal.

I came across an online article titled "Innovative Ways to Propose to Your Man This Leap Year," and it perfectly captures the thoughts of many women on this matter. One lady replied quite bluntly: "There is only one way to propose to a man: NEVER!'"

Let me ask you this: imagine yourself sitting in a restaurant and witnessing a woman getting down on one knee to propose to her partner. What would be your genuine reaction?

Throughout history, and even in present times, women have been known to be selective when it comes to choosing a partner. This instinct is deeply rooted in them and has spanned thousands of years. Women have an innate desire to protect their reproductive resources, often without even realising it.

When it comes to having babies, women have a unique experience. We carry a baby for nine months and can have a limited number of children in our lifetime. Men, on the other hand, don't have those same limitations, do they? Genetically speaking, they can be involved with multiple partners at once (and I know quite a few who are) and can potentially father limitless babies each year!

That's why men tend to be less picky when choosing a partner. In relationships, we usually place a lot of emphasis on emotions and carefully consider our options. On the other hand, men tend to have a more relaxed approach and enjoy exploring different options.

When we women trust our gut feelings and make choices, various behaviours can come into play. Some of these include:

- Challenging their man.
- Playing hard to get.
- Making the guy feel like they're in a friendly competition to catch their attention.

We often do these things without realising it (think about it). However, it's important to remember that not all women exhibit these actions, as every individual is different. But I bet you've already caught yourself doing a few of those things on that list, am I right?

"So, what has changed?"

Well, let's not overlook the fact that in the past, women were coyer and were pursued by men. She would decide if he would 'catch her'. It was rare to see a woman chase after a guy. This is where things get messed up, and this is where a lot of confusion arises!

Nowadays, it seems like the roles I just mentioned have been mixed up or reversed in some way! Have you noticed a shift where women are now pursuing the men, and women have started to take the lead in courtship? Women are now feeling the pressure to make men show interest in them while still retaining the power to decide whether or not to have sex. It seems that men are now determining if a relationship develops.

"How did this happen?"

Well, I've had conversations with many female clients and friends who have opened up about the lengths they go to impress men. They often pretend to be someone they're not, dressing up in clothes they wouldn't normally wear, acting overly sexy, and faking interest in the guy's hobbies, all in the hopes of making a connection. However, it's crucial to recognise that this role reversal shouldn't have happened in the first place, and that's where the problems arise. Allow me to elaborate further:

It seems that in recent years, women have lost sight of their inherent strengths. We are allowing our emotions and the overwhelming desire for a partner to take control.

We are constantly bombarded with articles urging us to break free from outdated notions and pursue the guys we're interested in. They tell us it's perfectly acceptable to ask a guy out and make the first move. Now, let me be clear—I am a strong woman who firmly believes that women can rule the world. However, I want to highlight the fact that by pursuing guys and taking the lead, we may be overlooking the innate advantages we have in the dating game. Trust me, it's a HUGE mistake! Allow me to explain...

Sometimes, our desire for love and a serious relationship can cause us to overlook our inbuilt instinct to find the perfect partner. As a result, men are now finding themselves in a position where they're being pursued by women instead of doing the pursuing. This shift from the traditional dynamic can sometimes create uneasiness and even decrease attraction. I see this happening frequently!

In primitive relationships, men were traditionally the hunters, and women were often seen as their prizes. There is an old-school dating rule that suggests men should take on the responsibility of asking women out, planning the date, and paying the bill – essentially doing all the heavy lifting. Many traditionally masculine men were content with this arrangement, until recent radical changes brought about a new evolution in our dating culture. Now, things have shifted, it is somehow accepted that women can chase men and insist on paying the bill themselves.

In my opinion, this is not necessarily a positive development. But before you get too shocked, let me explain, ladies... Keep an open mind.

I've noticed that my female clients and friends can easily get swept up in the excitement and chemistry of a new relationship with a guy. It's almost like they're under a spell, completely infatuated. And the more infatuated they become, the more they find themselves chasing after him. It's quite common for women to be the ones doing all the chasing, even if there hasn't been much progress in bringing them closer or building a future together.

"But how do men REALLY feel when a woman takes the lead in pursuing them?"

Some guys may claim to enjoy being chased, but deep down, do they truly feel that way? You'll be surprised, girls, but many guys I've talked to admit that they feel less attracted when women chase them. It's clear that men who see themselves as hunters prefer the thrill of the chase before claiming their well-deserved prize.

When a girl takes the initiative and asks a guy out, some guys might feel a bit threatened by her confidence. Chances are he'll say yes, go on the date, and might even let the lady pick up the tab. Sadly, this could lead to him losing interest after just one date (I've seen that happen far too often, not to be true).

You know what? I've realised that it's not always right for women to be the ones doing all the pursuing. By 'pursuing,' I mean taking the initiative, asking him out repeatedly, and constantly initiating messaging him while he only responds vaguely. Just a friendly reminder, ladies, chasing after a man can be a turn-off for many men. When a man pursues a woman, it comes from a place of masculinity.

You might think this sounds a bit old-school or not 'with the times", but men naturally enjoy the thrill of pursuit. It's in their DNA; it gets their blood pumping, and (they won't admit this freely) they like not knowing where they stand with you.

Guys will NEVER admit this to you, but they appreciate the idea of putting in effort to win your heart. (The saying 'What is worth having, is hard to get" comes to mind). You may come across men who claim that "it's fantastic when a woman takes the lead". However, usually, only lazy guys make such statements. Let's be honest, do we really want a lazy partner?

Do we want to take on the role traditionally associated with men in a relationship? Trust me, we all deserve a partner who puts in the effort. It's natural for us to want to be pursued, just as it's natural for men to want to pursue.

Often, when a woman takes the initiative and pursues a man, some guys may perceive it as being too needy or desperate, or, worst of all, 'easy'. And you know what? It ends up pushing away decent guys or, even worse, attracting those guys who just want 'fun' i.e., a quick hook-up with no strings, and they might try to take advantage of you. (There are plenty of guys out there like this). In my opinion, it's beneficial for women to embrace their feminine energy (more on this later) in a relationship and allow the masculine energy to take the lead.

Most guys tend to find more satisfaction in relationships when they actively pursue someone and go through a "chase" phase. They often fall in love with women who make them work for their affection. These men place less importance on relationships where intimacy, both emotional and physical, happens quickly and easily.

If you've ever tried to initiate a date or pursued a guy, you probably know it can leave you with a sour taste and set the tone for the relationship. How often has pursuing a guy turned out positively for you?

Here's a prime example: When I'm browsing online and come across a lovely pair of shoes, I think to myself, "Wow, they're beautiful!" and click on the link. However, if I see that they're on sale for £9.99, I start to question my initial impression. I take a closer look and realise they're not as magical as they appeared at first glance, so they lose their special appeal. If I were to buy them anyway, I would wear them once and then toss them to the bottom of my wardrobe.

However, if I clicked on that link and discovered that the same shoes were designer and cost £1,500, my desire for them would only grow stronger. I would be willing to work hard and save diligently to buy them. Once I owned them, I would cherish them and take great care of them. After wearing them, I would make sure to carefully place them back in their beautiful box.

"So, how does that compare to meeting a new guy?"

Well, my lovely, it's important to remember that what comes easily is not as valuable as what is harder to achieve. You need to learn to be those designer shoes!

Meeting and falling in love are often portrayed in romantic books and movies. From a young age, we are led to believe that love is blind, that a prince can fall in love with a pauper, and that love can overcome any obstacle. It's a topic that has captured the hearts and minds of many throughout history. Yes, books and movies have certainly played a role in shaping our perceptions of love. They often depict these star-crossed lovers who defy societal norms and overcome all odds in the name of love.

But WHOA! ... Let's be real here for a moment. Love is indeed a powerful force, but it doesn't always turn a blind eye to reality. Falling in love can be an exhilarating experience; there is no doubt about it. However, it doesn't guarantee that everything will magically work out or that every obstacle will simply disappear. While there are tales of princes falling for paupers and couples triumphing against all odds, those are the exceptions rather than the rule.

Relationships require effort, commitment, and compromise from both parties involved. Love can give you butterflies in your stomach and make you feel like you're on cloud nine. However, successful relationships are built on trust, communication, shared values, and mutual respect. So, while we can appreciate the romantic notions depicted in books and movies (because who doesn't love a good love story?), let's also remember that real-life relationships aren't always as perfect or easily resolved as they seem on screen (sadly).

In conclusion, love is indeed a beautiful thing that can unite people, even in challenging times. However, with online dating being the primary way to meet someone nowadays, it feels less like stumbling upon love and more like shopping for a partner. It's now as easy as flipping through an Argos catalogue and choosing solely based on appearances. "Oh, I like that one." "Oh wait, that one's even better!" Urgh!!

Of course, a woman can approach a man who may not initially be interested and win him over. It sounds good in theory, but things don't always work out that way. I've seen this happen time and time again.

I asked some of my girlfriends and female clients about their thoughts on pursuing men, and here are a few of their responses.

"I have no problem with asking men out, and I used to do it often when I was younger. However, I've learned from experience that many men will say 'yes,' even if they're not genuinely interested, just hoping for a chance to have sex. It's a waste of both your time and theirs. Nowadays, I would prefer not to ask a man out on a date, as I find it more preferable to engage in other activities."

Sammie ~33

"Pursuing a guy and putting in all the effort can be incredibly exhausting. Just imagine how you would feel being with someone who didn't even want you in the first place. Furthermore, you might start to wonder if he'll abandon you once you reduce your efforts to pursue him, and the benefits for him diminish. Trust me, sis, it's never worth it."

Hollie ~ 30

"Chasing a guy can get positive results, but it can also have the opposite effect and put you at a disadvantage. Instead of positioning you as a proactive advocate for equality, some may perceive it as an act of desperation or even question if there is an issue with you."

Serena ~ 42

"I have learned my lesson and will never chase after a guy again. It makes me cringe when I think about the times that I did. After all, men tend to value things more when they have to work for them."

Tracy ~ 52

Chasing after a guy can lead to unhappiness for the woman and make the guy feel less masculine since he doesn't have to work for the prize … YOU! In my opinion, this is not a recipe for success. So, to the amazing lady reading this, don't dull your shine just to fit in with society's expectations of "girl power." It's all about finding happiness while staying true to yourself, and you deserve to be pursued and wanted. *Oh, and I must say... If you want to pursue a guy, it's entirely your decision; you have every right to. I fully support your choice!*

Now, let's discuss how men decide whether to pursue you…

CHAPTER

6

"The Gatekeepers"

*A*h, the age-old debate about gender roles in sex and relationships. You know, there's a saying that **"women are the gatekeepers of sex, while men are the gatekeepers of commitment."** While there may be some truth to these claims, it's important to remember that these generalisations oversimplify the complex nature of human interactions and dynamics. So, let's dive deeper into this topic, shall we?

If you've ever found yourself in a situation where things didn't work out with a guy, you may have noticed that men have their approach to commitment. It's interesting how they often prefer to take things at their own pace in relationships, which can be quite different from how we approach them.

**Spoiler Alert: Just a head up, even if he feels a connection with you, it doesn't necessarily mean he's looking for a serious relationship. (Frustrating, right?!) Men often take their time to realise if they want something serious with a woman or how a relationship fits into their lives.

Sometimes, guys don't even realise they're searching for a relationship until they stumble upon one! They're not necessarily going around thinking, "Yep, having a partner would change my life for the better!" But here's the twist: he falls head over heels for this remarkable woman he's been hanging out with. Suddenly, it hits him – she's truly one in a million and impossible to replace. This is where you've got to make sure he realises that he wouldn't have had such a blast or incredible adventures with any other girl than YOU.

"But how do I do this?"

Basically, at the beginning, the idea is for him to be the one wondering if you're interested in a relationship. The key to creating attraction is to keep him slightly uncertain and curious. Here's the deal: he's trying to figure out if you're interested in him, but at the same time, he enjoys the excitement of not knowing where you stand in terms of a relationship. Don't let things move too quickly. You can let him know that you like him, but that doesn't mean you are ready to jump in bed with him.

Want to know the one thing that really kills attraction with guys and makes them run for the hills?

Well, it's when a woman appears desperate and overly clingy that things can become off-putting. This is especially true if the guy hasn't done anything to earn that level of devotion or if it's not reciprocated. Instead of evoking feelings of love and desire, it often just makes men feel guilty and burdened. To clarify, I am referring to those women who give up everything for their relationship, neglecting their friends and family to be solely with their partner. It is crucial not to go down this path, as it ultimately leads to unhappiness and anxiety.

It's a common pattern: many women can find themselves attracted to the wrong type of guy. Unfortunately, they often end up disappointed when the relationship falls apart or when they're treated poorly. Surprisingly, despite these negative experiences, they continue to be drawn to the same type of guy repeatedly. The problem is that if a woman dedicates herself SOLELY to a guy who doesn't deserve her, she may start behaving in unattractive ways, such as being possessive.

Constantly demanding his time and attention while neglecting her relationships and responsibilities can make guys think she's too clingy or needy. While men appreciate feeling wanted by women, they also want that connection to be earned. Acting overly needy with a guy who hasn't earned your undying loyalty will only make him lose interest quickly, trust me.

When it comes to dating and forming romantic connections, navigating the process can be quite tricky. From the initial attraction to developing a deep connection is an intricate journey. However, if we have a good understanding of the basic principles and patterns of human behaviour, we can approach these areas with more confidence and increase our chances of success. Essentially, it's about gaining insight into how that guy may think and feel.

The Key, when it comes to dating, is in the steps you take to capture someone's attention and win them over. Attraction is not solely dependent on looks and body language alone. If you reflect on past experiences when you were genuinely attracted to or in love with someone, I can confidently say that I bet it wasn't solely based on their physical appearance alone. It's a delightful combination of various factors – engaging conversations, shared funny moments, and maybe even their unique quirks or some of the traits that they would see as their 'faults', like their cackly laugh, their dark sense of humour or their love of Harry Potter.

Certain signals have the power to ignite that special spark within each of us. Creating a bond is all about establishing a deep emotional connection with someone. It's that incredible feeling when you simply click with someone on a whole new level. We all know how amazing (and rare) that feels!

Whether it's a romantic relationship or a close friendship, building a strong bond that leads to a committed relationship takes:

- Trust.
- Communication.
- Mutual respect.
- Shared life values.

Without ALL those elements, your chances of that relationship working are slim.

Once we start recognising the typical male behaviour, it becomes easier to make wise decisions about whom we choose to hang out with and how we build relationships. It's all about being more selective and investing our time only in meaningful connections.

Taking the time to select the right partner is way more crucial than you might think. It can determine whether your life is a dream... or a nightmare! **Read that again!**

When we have a clear understanding of our desires, goals, and approach relationships with the right mindset, we are giving ourselves the opportunity to find a perfect match. However, it all starts with self-reflection and looking at yourself. Allow me to explain this further...

CHAPTER
7

"Believe in your own value…"

*N*ever forget that what you put out into the universe, you'll attract back. Your ideal man is out there, searching for a woman he can shower with love while receiving the same in return. And guess what? That could very well be you! But do you place enough value on yourself?

I know that each of us has our own unique personality, preferences, opinions, and things that resonate with us or make us laugh. However, there are certain qualities that all remarkable women have in common. These qualities include:

- Self-Confidence.
- Independence.
- Integrity.
- Femininity.

Having a healthy amount of self-belief is what truly makes a woman stand out to a guy. However, it's important to remember that there's a fine line between being confident and coming across as arrogant. After all, nobody likes a show-off.

Guys who are genuinely interested in a serious relationship are attracted to women who value themselves and have strong boundaries. They want to feel like they have won a prize! No man wants someone who is easily manipulated unless he is solely focused on his interests. Women with loose boundaries can be easily influenced by men who are not truly interested in them. These women often go to great lengths to please everyone and seek approval, ultimately becoming known as 'Little Miss Pleaser'. So, you must avoid falling into that pattern.

Lean in; I have a juicy secret to share – high-quality men aren't looking for a woman they can trample on like yesterday's newspaper. Where's the excitement in that? You see if you're constantly trying to please him at the expense of your own happiness, you might just end up being taken advantage of. It's as if you're telling yourself, "If I'm as sweet as Treacle and ignore my own desires for his sake, he'll do the same for me." This is categorically NOT the case!

Sometimes, he might not meet a need that you never clearly mentioned to him, or he may cross a boundary that you didn't set. We all wish that people would always act how we'd like, but that's just wishful thinking. If you're constantly accommodating him without setting your own standards and clear expectations, it will only result in constant disappointment. Even the good guys you date will eventually get bored because they'll see how little attention you pay to your own wants and needs, and if you do not value yourself, then why the hell would HE (or anyone else) value you?

The goal is to be affectionate, genuine, and loving towards a man while also ensuring that he doesn't take advantage of you. Being assertive is crucial when it comes to dealing with men and building healthy relationships. And you know what? Confident men find assertive women quite appealing because they appreciate that these women know their worth and what they want in a partner. Assertive women can effectively set boundaries and handle disagreements with grace. Women who possess these qualities demonstrate emotional maturity and are adept at navigating challenging situations and disagreements with men, without resorting to being overly pushy or manipulative.

It is SO important that you never give up your true passions in life just to please a guy. No matter how amazing you think he is, never settle or compromise who you are just for the sake of being in a relationship. Men aren't looking for women who sacrifice everything for them. Remember, your self-respect should always come before your relationship status. It's not cool to change who you are or compromise your values just to please a guy. It's unattractive and, honestly, not worth it. By doing that, you're basically saying that your own beliefs and priorities mean very little. In my opinion, we women shouldn't have to sacrifice important parts of ourselves just to keep a man interested.

So, here's the bottom line: don't pretend to be someone you're not or compromise your desires just to win someone over or keep a guy around. Whether it's your dream of having seven kids in the future or your strong religious beliefs, don't discard them to fit in with a guy who doesn't want children. It's not worth sacrificing your happiness and dignity for the sake of someone else. It's important to steer clear of guys who try to pressure you into giving up those things. Your values and priorities should never be compromised for anyone!

"But how do I put this into action?"

It all begins with getting to know yourself better – understanding what YOU truly want, what you value, and where you set your boundaries. When you have a deep understanding of yourself, it can greatly influence how you communicate and live your daily life.

I can tell you that when a woman knows her worth, she shines with an undeniable confidence; she becomes a force of nature. She's got it all figured out – she embraces her awesomeness, acknowledges her strengths, and knows exactly what she deserves. This strong self-esteem affects every area of her life. If things aren't going well in a relationship, she won't hesitate to speak up or gracefully walk away if it doesn't meet her standards. This needs to be YOU, my darling, and it really can be!

You need to be self-assured.

"What does self-assured look like?"

Well, a self-assured lady can handle social situations like a master, even if she's a bit shy; when she socialises, she radiates confidence and doesn't waste time comparing herself to other women or trying to fit in. She doesn't let others dictate what she does. It doesn't bother her if another woman turns heads because of her attractiveness – it doesn't make her feel bad about herself. She understands that there will always be wealthier, slimmer, smarter, younger, and more good-looking women, but she's thankful that those things don't matter. Shallow stuff doesn't faze her. Whether a guy is good-looking, rich, or has high status, it doesn't bother her. She knows her worth goes way beyond all of that.

If you feel insecure about your appearance, let me assure you that finding love is not based on your looks. It's a subjective experience that differs from person to person. So, don't worry; your worth and the love you receive are not tied to external factors. I've personally witnessed individuals in their eighties, like my mum Hilda, who exuded more vitality and passion at the age of 80 than some people in their twenties. When you hit your forties, you might start missing the energy you had in your thirties. And when you reach your seventies, memories of your vibrant fifties may come flooding back. Whether you see yourself as young or old, time will always remind us that getting older is a present that is not gifted to all.

If you feel self-conscious about how you look, honey, trust me, in 20 or 30 years, you'll look back at pictures of yourself as you look today, and you will see just how young and beautiful you are right this minute! It's dumbfounding to think about how much time we waste dwelling on our perceived flaws and limitations instead of wholeheartedly pursuing our dreams.

In a nutshell, stop beating yourself up and remember, it comes down to being selective! When you have a fulfilling life, you won't feel the need to search for a man just to fill a void or make you happy. Having more options allows you to be more particular about whom you spend time with. With a fulfilling and amazing life, you'll find it much easier to make wise decisions when choosing a partner.

"So, why is it so important to be confident?"

Well, let me tell you, when a man comes across a strong, independent woman, he's usually very intrigued and wants to be a part of her world. He wants to be a part of her amazing life, but he's also not afraid that she'll become too clingy. Many guys have this common fear in relationships, where they worry about feeling suffocated and losing their freedom. They're afraid that being in a relationship means sacrificing their independence.

Alright, come closer. I've got a big secret to tell you... Men fall in love with the woman who inspires them to become the best version of themselves, the woman who makes them feel like a true MAN! He needs to know that you're not asking him to change who he is; instead, you're accepting him for who he is and inviting him to be a part of your amazing life. Finding that perfect balance and ensuring he feels valued and included is crucial. It's beneficial for both of you if he has his hobbies and interests. This can make your relationship healthier and more balanced.

If there are activities he's not really into, such as Zumba, wine tasting, shopping, or chilling with your friends, don't force him to do them. Everyone should be able to enjoy what they like! Don't worry, you can still engage in those activities without him and be happy. There will always be some hobbies that are his alone, and some things that you enjoy but he doesn't, and that is fine!

When conflicts arise (because they often do), try to resolve them by having open conversations instead of blaming or becoming defensive, moody, or passive-aggressive (which can be a huge turn-off). Instead of simply trying to 'win' the argument or prove that you are right, and he is wrong, try to understand and listen. He will listen to you more if you listen to him more, BINGO!

Remember that relationships are constantly evolving, so it's important to maintain open lines of communication. If you want a strong and long-lasting relationship, both parties need to be committed and put in the effort. Every challenge that comes your way is an opportunity for personal growth and can bring people closer together. So, it's a win-win situation for everyone involved!

The key is to find the perfect balance between independence and making him feel valued for what he brings to the table. It can be a bit challenging, but it's 100% worth considering.

With the right knowledge and approach, you have the power to create deep connections built on:

- *Love.*
- *Trust.*
- *Respect.*
- *Understanding.*

It's a wise move to show a guy that you're genuinely paying attention to his actions and personality. One way to do this is by asking light-hearted questions. It shows your interest in getting to know him better and creates a fun way to engage with him. It also lets him know that you're genuinely interested in learning more about him. However, remember to ask these questions with confidence and playfulness.

I gave this exact advice to one of my clients who felt like her relationship was becoming distant and stagnant. She decided to put this method into action, and I received an email from her (with her permission to share).

"Hey, Kel, so here is an update on how it went last night ...

I prepared a cosy dinner at home, complete with his favourite meal and a bottle of wine. As we sat down at the table, I started asking him unexpected questions that caught him off guard.

"Alright, bubs," I said playfully. "If you were an animal, which one do you think best represents your personality?" He chuckled and pondered for a moment before replying, "Definitely a lion! Strong, confident, and fiercely protective."

While we continued our meal, I asked him more questions that made him reflect on his personality traits. We started with silly hypothetical scenarios, like which superpower he would choose (he went with teleportation because he hates traffic).

Then, we moved on to more thought-provoking questions about his dreams and aspirations.

With each question, I could see his eyes light up as he shared more about himself. It was as if me asking these questions made him feel seen and appreciated. But it wasn't just about the questions; it was about the genuine interest that drove them. I listened intently to each answer as we discussed, asking follow-up questions and engaging in meaningful conversations sparked by his responses. It was incredibly interesting, and I discovered so much about him (and vice versa).

As the evening went on, we spoke about deeper topics – discussing our fears, sharing childhood stories, and even confessing hidden quirks we had never revealed before. The atmosphere was filled with laughter and vulnerability. I was so shocked, Kel!

By the end of the night, we both felt closer than ever before. It was clear that these simple questions had opened up avenues for us to connect on a deeper level. So, the light bulb in my brain went off when I realised that genuinely caring about each other's lives is like a secret recipe for a healthy and thriving relationship. Thank you so much x"!

I can tell you straight, that if you approach a guy with fear or anxiety, it shouldn't come as a surprise if he mirrors your energy and responds negatively. His reaction could range from withdrawing to becoming irritated. However, when you handle situations in a confident and light-hearted manner, it sends a clear message that you are not simply waiting for a guy to choose you. It demonstrates that you have your own standards and expectations for how people should behave. Men tend to notice and appreciate this quality.

When you make the decision to take control of your dating and love life, it's important to approach it with care. Instead of using manipulative tactics (which men can spot easily and find off-putting), try maintaining an optimistic and self-assured attitude. This will create a much healthier and more authentic experience. Being clear about what you want in a relationship sends a clear message to the guy without being overly assertive. It shows that you are confident, well-informed, and making decisions based on your own knowledge, which will make him feel like he's found a valuable partner.

Trust your instincts and exercise good judgment. The interesting aspect is that when men become aware that women are actively selecting and evaluating their qualities, it sends a subconscious message to them, resulting in a completely different experience with them. Naturally, men have a need to feel masculine. Allow me to explain further...

CHAPTER

8

"Never 'settle'"

$\mathcal{I}$t's important to understand that maintaining composure, displaying confidence, and exercising personal control can make you more attractive to men. It demonstrates that you have faith in yourself and are not easily swayed by external factors. While some may perceive having standards as being overly picky, it's about finding a balance between knowing what you want and not settling for just anyone who happens to be available.

Having standards does not make you shallow, foolish, or a hopeless dreamer. Having standards can save you time in the long run if you are realistic about the expectations you have for your potential partner.

Maintaining high standards simply means not settling for anything less than a person who consistently brings a smile to your face, demonstrates kindness, supports you in every way, cares about your interests (even if they don't share them), and genuinely cares about you. It's all about finding someone who meets all the necessary criteria!

"Is physical attraction important?"

Well. I often find that my initial impression of someone's attractiveness doesn't hold up over time. It seems that the more I get to know someone, the more attractive they become to me. Their personality and confidence have a significant impact on their appeal. Surprisingly, many of my exes didn't catch my eye right away, but as I got to know them better, they became incredibly attractive to me. That just goes to show that attraction goes beyond physical appearance.

The key to letting a man know that you're the one making the choice is to communicate it in the right way, triggering a deep response inside him that will make him see you as a long-term partner. Think of the common phrase "make an honest woman of her." That's when a guy transitions from casually dating a woman to desiring a long-term future with her.

It's pretty crazy how life can unexpectedly change! Out of nowhere, this guy's perspective on the woman completely flips. Suddenly, he realises how amazing their relationship is and wants to fully commit for the long term. It's like he's eager to make things official with you as soon as possible.

When it comes to relationships, your behaviour and characteristics play a vital role in catching a guy's attention. It's all about how you carry yourself and what makes you unique. These signals basically tell him how much you're into him. It tells him this lady isn't interested in anything casual, so if he wants to keep her around, he had better step up his game and meet her standards!

Remember, you never get a second chance to make a first impression! The way you initially interact with a guy can greatly influence his behaviour and perception of acceptable behaviour in future interactions. Therefore, it's incredibly important to start things off on the right note and set clear expectations for how he should act from the beginning. There is NO rewind button in life… READ THAT AGAIN!

STOP:

1. Chasing after men who are not showing interest or making serious effort with you. Don't make excuses for their behaviour. If it ends up turning into a relationship,

trust me, it will be a lousy one. Do you want that? Do you want to be in a relationship where you like him more than he likes you, and he's just half-assing it? *Spoiler Alert: You deserve the WHOLE ASS!!!

2. Posting stories or photos on your social media/WhatsApp etc, just to get that dopamine hit when you see him watching or liking them (and feel a bit disappointed when he still doesn't contact you or make the effort). By doing this, you will constantly seek his validation. Don't give that kind of power to a guy who doesn't deserve you.

3. Cyberstalking him and trying to "figure" him out on social media. He should be sharing details of his life with you openly and willingly, and it is not your business to be prying into his life before he is ready. How would you like it if it was the other way around? Red Flag!

4. Putting up with his hot and cold behaviour just because he is 6ft 2" and has a great car Well, he could be any height, but let's be honest, an asshole is an asshole, even if he drives a Bentley! Don't let that set the standard for how a man should treat you.

5. Accepting Netflix & Chill plans. Know your worth and values. Say no to hook-ups and "hanging out". You can never be too discerning when it comes to men.

When you approach a new relationship in the right way, it can have a powerful impact on someone's psyche, particularly for guys. It has the potential to bring you closer together and create a stronger sense of connection by building trust. So, let's dive in and explore this further.

CHAPTER

9

"Miss Right or Miss Right-Now?"

S o, here's the secret sauce... When a guy is really into you, he will imagine you in one of two different ways in his mind.

Either he will see you as someone he could potentially date and have a serious, long-term relationship with, including marriage and children. In other words, he views you as someone who fulfils all the criteria for a committed relationship, and in his eyes, you are essentially marriage material.

Or:

He finds you attractive without much emotional connection. It's more about the physical aspect, having a good time, and keeping things casual rather than forming any deep emotional bond, like a friends-with-benefits situation.

These two scenarios are complete opposites in a man's mind. Essentially, he will see you as either Miss Right or Miss Right-Now. It is crucial to remember that a guy's desire for physical intimacy doesn't necessarily indicate his search for a serious relationship. It's important to avoid jumping to conclusions and assuming that physical intimacy automatically implies commitment. READ THAT AGAIN!

Men can sometimes be fickle when it comes to dating. They can quickly shift from considering a woman as "the one" to casually seeing her until they find someone that they feel more compatible with, without much difficulty.

But...

Transitioning from being someone's 'Miss Right-Now' to becoming their "Miss Right" and finding a meaningful relationship may not be an easy journey. It can be challenging for a guy to change his perspective, but it's possible when he meets someone who he values for more than just their looks. In short, if you're looking for a potential long-term relationship, it's crucial not to start off as 'Miss Right-Now.'

The thing is, if you are seeking a genuine and committed relationship, it is crucial to communicate that clearly. Let him know from the start what you are looking for if you think he has potential. If he sees you as a 'casual' or 'fun only' girl, chances are you will always stay in that category. Setting the right expectations through open and honest communication is key. If you see potential with a guy, it is important to let him know upfront that you are serious about finding something meaningful and that you are not a woman who settles for less. Being girlfriend material involves being open, honest, and ensuring that he understands your morals.

Do you believe that jumping in the sack is the key to capturing a guy's attention and keeping it? Do you think that establishing a "friends-with-benefits" arrangement and fostering a casual "situationship" is the most effective approach to gaining his attention and making him develop feelings for you?
NOPE!!

Listen, a girl has needs. So, if ALL you want is physical intimacy and you are down for that, then carry on, and good for you! But if, deep down, you're secretly hoping he'll realise he loves you and wants you as his serious girlfriend, then you are setting yourself up for potential serious disappointment.

The simple truth is that building a connection solely based on sexual desires is rather pointless. While it may seem tempting in the short term and it may scratch an itch, it rarely leads to anything meaningful and leaves you feeling unsatisfied. I understand that some women do this out of fear and insecurity. They worry about scaring a guy off by discussing the idea of taking their relationship to the next level or feel uncomfortable talking about long-term commitments.

It might seem like the only option is to try even harder and give it your all, hoping to make this guy fall for you. However, if you've been down this road before, you know how frustrating and unproductive it can be. It also smashes your self-esteem even further down. That's why it is incredibly important for you to know exactly what you want and to establish clear personal boundaries when interacting with men. Do not make excuses simply because a guy is attractive, successful, wealthy, or comes from a certain background. You will only be treated the way you allow, so stay true to your principles and refuse to accept wishy-washy behaviour. Essentially, avoid situations where the other person benefits while you end up losing out.

In fact, if a woman has strong personal boundaries and a good moral compass, she will not put herself in a dating situation that is solely advantageous for either herself or the man. There may be moments when she could easily exploit a man and come out on top, but if her values are high, she is less likely to pursue that path because she understands that healthy relationships should always be mutually beneficial.

If you want to succeed with guys, it's crucial to establish clear boundaries and know when to confidently say "NO," step back, or move on from a relationship that lacks balance. It can be confusing for some women when they come across conflicting advice about playing games in relationships. The confusion often arises from not understanding the underlying meaning behind the "hard-to-get" concept.

"So, is it not a good idea to play hard to get?"

94

Well, let me break it down for you: The truth is, genuine, good guys aren't interested in women who pretend to be uninterested, are unreliable, or play mind games just to keep them hooked. What they really admire are women who don't tolerate wasting time or being manipulated. They know exactly what they want and aren't afraid to say it.

Allow me to provide you with straightforward advice on how to improve your dating skills.

Firstly, avoid making the mistake of assuming you know what a guy wants simply based on a strong connection or amazing chemistry.

Secondly, just because a guy has a connection with you doesn't necessarily mean he wants to jump into a relationship or sees you as someone he would marry.

As women, we may sometimes struggle to fully understand a man's perspective and tend to accept it as it is, whether positive or negative. However, through extensive research, I have discovered that there is much more to this topic, and it is truly intriguing. So, let's delve into it.

CHAPTER

10

"Only fools rush in."

$\mathcal{I}$t's unfair to stereotype all men as sex-crazed beasts, always on the prowl for a new conquest, incapable of committing to a relationship. We should not hold onto the myth that men only want one thing...

"But that is true, guys ARE only after one thing... How can you say differently?"

Well, let me explain it like this: Guys are looking for more than just physical intimacy. They do want a deeper connection with a woman. When it comes to guys, let's be honest – they're usually initially drawn in by physical attraction. A guy can spot a woman who catches his eye and instantly be intrigued by her appearance alone, without any inclination to know more about her.

He will easily get involved with this woman, letting his physical desires take control without much thought or concern for the consequences or recklessness involved. He tends to get carried away with his primal urges and isn't considering any potential negative consequences at this stage. There are loads of guys out there who are only interested in a woman's appearance and the sexual relationships they could have with her. I'm sure most of you reading this will be nodding in agreement right now.

Essentially, what is happening is that men's instincts for physical attraction have a significant influence on their decision-making. This is because their emotional sensitivity is not as pronounced as that of women. I have observed this phenomenon a few times, where a man begins dating an incredibly attractive woman, and his friends are amazed, thinking how fortunate he is. However, as time passes, reality sets in, and they realise that she is a nightmare dressed as a daydream. Suddenly, those same friends start wondering how he can tolerate her.

The woman in question may have been causing a lot of trouble, displaying mean and deceitful behaviour. However, the guy either didn't catch on, or he did but didn't care, as the sexual attraction was off the scale (i.e., she was super-hot). What's happening here, apart from some men being completely oblivious, is that they become so consumed by their intense physical attraction that they neglect their deeper desires for long-term happiness and simply go with the flow in the moment with no thought to the future at all. They are not even thinking of the true importance of a fulfilling relationship.

Typically, after a few months, dopamine levels drop, and the initial intense physical attraction fades. It is at this point that the man gains clarity and begins to recognise all the warning signs about the woman in front of him, which others had been cautioning him about. It's like a massive wake-up call for him! Shortly after, the relationship ends, and the man starts questioning his judgment, saying things like, 'How could I have dated her?' or 'What was I thinking?'

That's why it's crucial for you to not rush into a relationship solely based on a strong sexual connection with him. It's important to exercise caution and avoid risking your heart for a guy who may only be interested in the physical attraction they feel. Trust me, taking this approach can lead to disastrous outcomes (been there, done that).

You must have heard of The Honeymoon Phase.

The honeymoon phase occurs in the first few months after meeting someone and is characterised by a rush of neurotransmitters that make us feel "in love." It's like a natural high that gradually fades over time. During this period, we often focus on the present rather than the future. However, true compatibility goes beyond just good sex or the initial feeling of attraction.

Sometimes, you'll find that once the endorphin rush fades away, a relationship won't last if there aren't any common interests or relationship goals. It takes time to truly get to know someone, and rushing into a relationship is like playing chicken on the motorway. People change, that's just a fact of life. The real test is whether the relationship can adapt to these changes, resolve conflicts, and, most importantly, compromise.

When we first enter a new relationship, everything feels exciting and fresh. At this point, you're fuelled by oxytocin, the powerful hormone that creates sexual attraction and the euphoric feeling of new romance. We try to show the best version of ourselves.

However, as time goes by, we often become complacent. It's just human nature. The six-month mark is significant because it signifies a shift into a new phase. You may project onto your partner the positive qualities you desire, seeing them more as you want them to be rather than as they truly are.

Reaching the half-year mark is a big deal. It means you've really seen them, warts and all, you're not just smitten anymore, you've got to grips with who they really are. You're seeing each other through a much sharper lens now so it is easier to work out if you are a good fit.

Think of it this way: starting a new job is exciting and great. However, after six months, it can easily become just another job. If you approach each day at work with the same enthusiasm as your first day, you're more likely to succeed. On the other hand, if you start slacking off and sleeping in after your probation period, chances are you won't last long. The same principle applies to relationships.

That's why it's important not to rush in too fast. Take the time to see if both of you are willing to go the extra mile to make it work and, more importantly, if you are compatible. It is important to try to maintain at least some of the initial effort and enthusiasm that you put into the relationship and not just start taking it for granted. Assuming it will all stay fine is a big mistake and often leads to a breakup.

I've noticed that many women tend to rush into things with a guy without thinking. This is something I often see happening with my clients who get carried away with a strong connection and chemistry, it is also why they end up having to employ me!

Let's explore this topic further...

CHAPTER

11

"Connection & Chemistry"

I often hear my clients and friends talk about the chemistry or connection they feel with a new guy they've met. We use these terms to describe a special and unique feeling towards someone, which is quite rare. However, it's important to remember that sometimes, we may assign our own interpretations to it without checking if the man feels the same way. This is a BIG mistake (YUP, I learned the hard way).

Isn't it bloody hard to find a guy with whom you share that special chemistry? When we genuinely click with someone we like, it feels like hitting the jackpot because that kind of connection is rare. Have you ever caught yourself getting carried away and daydreaming about a future together just because the chemistry is off the scale? You don't even know this guy properly, but you are already wondering how your name would look with his surname!

I have learned (once again, the hard way) that men and women experience attraction in very different ways. While women often associate physical and chemical attraction with deeper, long-term connections, the same may not be true for men.

Many women, at some point, find themselves:
1. Dealing with liars and manipulators.
2. Being unceremoniously dumped out of the blue.
3. Not getting the commitment they desire.

It feels like an endless cycle, and it's frustrating. This situation happens more often than we care to admit.

Example of a dialogue I hear many times a week from coaching clients:

"We didn't really have much in common, except for this so-called 'connection' or 'chemistry'." To be honest, we were just completely different. We didn't share any common interests, values, or even the ability to have a decent conversation. There seemed to be no future for us as a couple.

I've been in this situation myself and witnessed many situations where women, even after dating for a short while, started enjoying just the sexual connection with the man they're with while failing to connect on a deeper level. **That's a huge red flag.** The connection and sexual attraction were the only things that existed, but the woman was still holding on tightly and refusing to let go of all the false meaning she had attached to the connection.

If love were solely based on appearances, we would find ourselves falling in love every time we passed an attractive person on the street. We might have experienced love at first sight multiple times by the time we got home. The truth behind this phenomenon is that our subconscious mind often compares a person's appearance or scent to someone significant from our past, instantly causing us to fall in love. This is why I could potentially experience love at first sight with someone, while you might only see them as ordinary.

In the early stages of love, people often put their partners on a pedestal, making them seem perfect and downplaying any flaws they might have. It's all part of the infatuation game 'have you ever found yourself doing that?

"Is it true that guys like girls who are 'one of the guys?

I'm not sure who came up with the idea that men want a woman who's essentially 'one of the guys', but I highly doubt it came from a man. Trying to blend in with the guys means adopting masculine attitudes, behaviours, and hobbies. It's not necessarily a bad thing, but if you're seeking romance and sexual chemistry with a guy, being too much like one of his pals might work against you.

It all comes down to how much a man is attracted to and emotionally connected with a woman. The more interested he is, the more attention she receives. Even if a woman considers herself "one of the guys," she can still attract and connect with a man to some extent. However, things might change if another woman who fully embraces her femininity and unique qualities enters the picture – she could quite literally steal the show!

Typically, straight guys (the ones you'd want to date, I assume) don't develop romantic feelings for their male friends. So, if you're seen only as a "guy friend," it will be challenging to catch the attention of women seeking male companionship. Women in this situation often find themselves trapped in the friend zone by the guys in their social circle. And there are two significant ways they inadvertently sabotage themselves.

First and foremost, if your male friends see you solely as one of the guys, they might not consider you as a potential romantic partner. Even if one of them does start dating you, the relationship may not progress further if they don't feel a strong attraction towards you. Secondly, always identifying with men can give off a "bro" vibe when meeting and dating men outside your social circle. This might convey a friendly or non-sexual energy, which may not be what guys are looking for.

If you're looking to grab a guy's attention and make him chase after you focus on becoming the type of woman, those men find irresistible. However, if you prefer a casual, less intense, strictly platonic relationship like the ones guys have with their buddies, then go ahead and be one of the guys. Just like any other dating advice, this isn't foolproof. There are exceptions to every rule. I'm sure you'll come across some ladies who have a "bro"-like mindset and are in happy relationships with men. So yeah, I'm not saying this applies to everyone without fail, but rather addressing what seems to be the general mindset of men when it comes to women and dating. The whole point of this book is to help you increase your chances of dating success!

"So, what does all of that really mean?"

For example, have you ever experienced that feeling when you meet someone and instantly become infatuated, only to later discover that they weren't as interested in you? It can be quite disappointing. Unfortunately, some guys view it as a game to woo and win over women, losing interest as soon as they 'win the game'. It's a sad reality. These men frequently enjoy sharing stories with their buddies about their conquests and discussing strategies to attract women and engage in casual encounters. You may have overheard men talking in this manner, and perhaps you have even heard men you know or men you have worked with speak like this… I know I have!

There are literally books upon books written by guys all about how to quickly pick up woman after woman and go from 'conquest' to 'conquest', basically how to be a player!

So, let's take a closer look at how to recognise these 'players' and separate them out from the guys looking for serious relationships o you know how to AVOID them.

CHAPTER

12

"Players, players everywhere!"

The word 'player' makes my skin crawl. At some point in our lives, we've all had the displeasure of encountering these so-called 'Players', be it within our circle of friends or in the dating scene. It's hardly a walk in the park, is it? However, it's crucial to understand that these players can be classified into three distinct categories. These are:

The Ego Driven Players

These guys certainly relish being in the spotlight, basking in the admiration of several ladies. It's a total ego lift for them. They likely have no ill intentions but trust me, they've mastered the art of flirtation and aren't shy about showing it off. They could sweet-talk even the birds from the trees! They're on a mission for compliments and validation from as many women as possible without caring how their behaviour might impact others.

They have a knack for establishing immediate, profound, and meaningful relationships with women. It's as though they possess a unique allure that encourages women to be open (and I mean entirely). However, here's the unexpected part – these men are often quite insecure beneath the surface and rely on female validation to bolster their self-esteem. So, stay alert! It might be time to step back if things begin to whirlwind at an alarming pace. Now, then, shall we proceed with the next group?

'Man About Town Players.

These chaps are truly masters in the art of charming women, and they've turned it into their favourite hobby. They're constantly on the move, never missing a step, and always seem to have a companion for every event. You won't catch them idling at home on a Saturday evening. Oh no, they'd much prefer to be out mingling with other sociable individuals who enjoy meeting new people, especially those of the opposite sex. And we mustn't overlook...

Sexually Charged Players

There are men out there who believe in creating a cosy atmosphere from the get-go, using body language and closeness as their tools. They're aware that establishing a connection through physical touch can be an effective way to win a woman's heart. However, their knack for boosting the morale of women who may be feeling insecure could make any potential separation even more challenging. So, trust me, it is wise to steer clear of these types if you can.

Isn't it just a bit of a let-down? You meet this wonderful man who exudes an undeniable charm and appears to tick all the boxes for an ideal boyfriend. But here's the catch: those very characteristics that draw you in may also mean he's not quite cut out for a profound, committed relationship. He might be missing those nurturing, giving, patient, courteous and thoughtful qualities we so desire. It's like he makes you feel amazing when you're with him, but as soon as you part ways, you're left feeling anxious and unsure.

Have you ever found yourself attracted to a strong, powerful man who seems out of reach? I totally get it (I've been there too)! The truth is, being attractive and intriguing doesn't necessarily mean someone would make a good partner. In fact, those types often turn out to be the opposite of what you truly need for a fulfilling and meaningful relationship.

If a guy you meet is honest about not looking for something serious or wanting to keep things casual from the start, it's important to BELIEVE HIM!! If you're seeking something deeper, it's clear that your preferences don't align.

When dealing with a guy who is solely focused on himself, it's likely that he will show selfish behaviour in all aspects of the relationship. Hangouts will always be on his terms, without considering your schedule or convenience. If you find yourself constantly playing the role of an entertainer instead of a friend, always needing to be "on" or else it becomes an issue, it's a clear sign of their self-centeredness. He only cares about your preferences, thoughts, and feelings if they align with his. He puts in the bare minimum effort for you and holds you to a standard that he never bothers to meet.

These players give genuinely nice guys a bad name. Believe it or not, there are men out there who are not players and genuinely want to be in a relationship with women. But here's the sad thing: many of these men lack the skills or experience needed to make that magical connection happen and will easily/often get outshined by the 'players' in the local bar or nightclub.

As a result, we women often miss out on finding real love simply because we don't feel those butterflies (don't worry, we'll talk about that later). If you come across a guy who thinks he's smooth with his cheesy lines and calculated moves, from smooth compliments to lingering eye contact and maybe even a touch of playful teasing, these moves are all part of their game. Keep your wits about you, and remember, all that glitters is not gold!

My suggestion? Stay away from these guys, no matter what. Trust me, I've learned this the hard way, too—it's a lose-lose situation.

"What if I really like him, but my gut tells me to run?"

Well, let me start by saying that if you browse through online dating advice forums, you'll notice a common pattern: women often seek aid after finding themselves in dating disasters. So, why does this happen? In most cases, it's because they ignored warning signs and that instinctive gut feeling that we all have. While it may be true that some women lower their standards or have none at all, it is important to acknowledge that there are also many who may not be fully in touch with their intuition.

In most cases, women have a gut feeling about whether a man is right or wrong for them. Even if we can't always pinpoint the exact reason, our instincts tend to guide us towards what is best for us. Trusting our intuition can lead us to healthier and more fulfilling relationships.

So, there was this thing he did that you weren't too fond of, but you brushed it off or ignored it and kept on dating him anyway. BIG mistake! Always trust your gut. Think of intuition as your own personal GPS, guiding you towards your desired destination. Trust those gut feelings that arise before your brain starts overthinking things. Your instincts are there for a reason and can often lead you in the right direction. So, don't ignore them!

"Tell me, how can I spot a player from a mile away?"

Alright, I can do that. Let's keep it simple. Here are a few signs to look out for when you first meet:

- When his words don't align with his actions.

- Making promises and never following through.
- Seeing you only when it's convenient for him.
- He has no interest in satisfying your sexual needs.
- He doesn't try to get to know you on a deeper level.
- He is always updating his social media but doesn't post about you, yet he posts other people.
- He only talks to you late at night when he is bored, lonely, or horny and never asks about you.

The list goes on... and on, but you get the gist.

If a guy is labelled a "player", it's not exactly a compliment. Let me tell you why. This tag is generally seen in a negative light because it suggests that he's not genuinely interested in building real connections with people. Instead, he relies on crafty tricks to win over your love interests.

Dealing with a guy who displays player-like behaviour can be emotionally devastating. It's important to remember that not everyone labelled as a player fits this exact description, as the term can have different interpretations depending on the situation. However, players are typically known for manipulating others for their own selfish gain. On the other hand, healthy and authentic relationships thrive on trust, respect, and open communication.

A genuine and honest relationship is built on caring for each other, being emotionally available, and wanting a deeper connection. That's why it's concerning when someone is labelled as a player – it makes you question their true intentions and whether they can form genuine relationships. It's smart to be cautious and pay attention to warning signs when it comes to dating and relationships. Don't ignore those red flags! Trust your instincts and protect that heart of yours.

Guys who use fake charm to hit on women often do it to boost their own ego and seek validation. They have no intention of committing or forming genuine connections. It doesn't matter how impressive or gorgeous a woman may be, as they don't truly care about her or have any interest in a relationship. These guys are all about the excitement of chasing after women, always looking for the next thrill. They crave instant gratification and have no interest in forming real connections because they think there's always someone better out there.

It's important to remember that a player's mindset has absolutely nothing to do with YOUR worth or appearance.

Don't bother wasting your time trying to change a guy like this, trust me. They are completely self-centred and unwilling to compromise. Players only care about satisfying their physical desires and boosting their ego by surrounding themselves with women. Don't be fooled by their empty words and shallow intentions – you deserve better than that. It's a losing game, my darling, and you are not a loser!

A player is defined as someone who has practised enough to appear sincere to multiple girls, leading them to believe him. He may lie, mislead, manipulate, and make you believe things that aren't true, all with the intention of getting intimate. This behaviour is something he has perfected and is skilled at. He may even come across as confident, cocky, smooth, and quick-witted (usually because of lots of practice).'

These guys believe that the best way for them to get in a woman's pants is to act as if they want a relationship with her. You won't be able to tell right away. You just must go on dates with a bunch of guys who look the same until you stumble upon a good one.

Sorry, but that's the truth.

Until you find that special someone to share your life with, it's important to learn how to find contentment in your own company and the companionship of your family and friends. Instead of settling for just ANY guy who shows interest or tries to please others, focus on building fulfilling relationships without compromising or negotiating. And remember, with a positive mindset, there are plenty of amazing guys out there who would be lucky to date you. Don't get caught up in FOMO – there are plenty of options to choose from! Plenty!!

Let's delve deeper into this…

CHAPTER 13

"Little Miss 'I Can Change Him'"

*Y*ou know, there are ladies out there (I've met a few) who believe they have this special power to "change" a player and make him appreciate a fantastic relationship. However, they often overlook who the man truly is. Let me tell you about my friend Lily. She used to think she could change a player until she was given a swift reality check.

Lily and Max unexpectedly crossed paths outside a charming local café. As they engaged in conversation, Lily found herself irresistibly drawn to Max's captivating charm and the glint in his eyes.

You see, Max had made it very clear to Lily that he was not looking for commitment. Max was just up for 'fun', and he had also divulged that he was not looking for a girlfriend and had, in fact, never had a girlfriend, as he likes to be a 'free bird'. But. Lily, being Lily, firmly believed that, deep down, he was capable of genuine love and commitment. With that in mind, despite her friends' advice to the contrary, Lily embarked on her quest to make Max realise that one woman was enough for him- and that woman was her!

Lily came up with a plan to spend more time with Max and show him the true meaning of love and commitment. From spontaneous picnics in Hyde Park to cosy movie nights at home, she showered him with affection and care. However, as time went on, Lily began to realise that she had taken on more than she had expected.

Max's charismatic nature remained unchanged; he continued to flirt with other women wherever they went. It seemed like, no matter what she did, she couldn't break through his walls and make him commit solely to her. Despite the setbacks, Lily refused to give up easily. She believed that deep down, there was a vulnerable side to Max that only needed the right person to unlock it, and that person was her! Along this roller coaster ride of emotions, unexpected twists awaited them both.

As time passed, Lily started feeling insecure and hurt as she saw Max receiving flirty texts from unknown numbers and going on mysterious late-night outings. Despite her efforts to change him, it seemed that Max's player nature was deeply ingrained.

Next, Lily introduced Max to one of her close friends. This friend had experienced heartbreak in the past but had now found love and happiness. Lily believed that seeing true love up close would awaken something inside Max and make him realise that he could have that same happiness with her. Unfortunately, Max sees it as an opportunity for another conquest and ends up making advances towards her friend.

Despite her best efforts, Lily couldn't deny that she had failed in her mission to reform Max's player ways. It was disheartening for her to witness someone so resistant to change and unable to appreciate genuine connections.

In the end, Lily realised that she couldn't fix Max. However, she did discover a newfound strength within herself. She learned to accept that some things are beyond her control and that it's okay to walk away from situations that don't help her.

Lily said goodbye to Max, knowing deep down that she had given her all. In doing so, she grew wiser and stronger. Now, Lily is happily married with twins and a wonderful husband.

Never forget that players are mainly focused on superficial matters. They prioritise appearances and instant gratification over genuine and meaningful connections (they enjoy the hunt too much). So, if you're looking for something authentic and deep, it's probably best to avoid them like the plague. When guys heavily rely on pickup techniques to attract women, it usually shows that they are not fully aligned in their lives and lack important connections.

"But wait, how can I know if he is genuine?"

So, here's the deal: I have said it before, and I will keep saying it … If a man says, "I'm not looking for anything serious" or "I'm just looking for something casual," BELIEVE HIM!! He genuinely wants to have a good time and isn't looking for someone to change him or make him fall in love. If you meet a guy who talks the talk but doesn't walk the walk, it means he's not internally aligned. His actions and ego are not in line with his true feelings. He seems disconnected from himself, which makes it difficult for him to be authentic and consistent in managing his thoughts, emotions, and overall well-being.

If a guy seems to be overly focused on sex, it's clear that he struggles to find a balance in life. He'll probably be completely clueless about his own emotions and simply pursue what he wants without considering the consequences. He may not even care or understand how you feel because his values and emotions are all mixed up. And, let's face it, men often have a reputation for being promiscuous, which is why women sometimes make mistakes when they're attracted to them.

There are plenty of self-absorbed men out there who can't seem to stop talking about themselves. I'm sure you've met a few in your lifetime. These men have a knack for creating an engaging personality that might initially appear intriguing or appealing. This kind of talk may be fun on a first date. However, it's important to be cautious, as it could all just be a temporary facade.

When a guy uses sarcasm, humour, and charm to manipulate another person, especially a woman, it can make her feel defensive. It's a sneaky tactic that is employed to divert your attention from objectively evaluating them. Their main aim is to manipulate women into disregarding their logical thinking and succumbing to irresistible attraction factors.

"Help me! Why do I keep choosing the wrong guys?"

Honestly, it's because you're stuck in a victim mindset. So, you'll continue to feel like a victim. Take some time to focus on yourself and boost your self-esteem. Reflect on what you truly want in a partner and why you're attracted to men who take advantage of you. It might be tough, but being brutally honest with yourself is definitely worth it. Many people want what they can't have because they've been told it's off-limits, while others are attracted to things they don't fully understand because they enjoy the process of discovering them.

Whether good or bad, the people you attract are reflecting something within yourself. However, it can be challenging to recognise the negative traits in yourself, which can lead to resentment towards certain individuals you attract into your life. Life is all about those good vibes and energy, you know? The way we present ourselves to the world is exactly how the world responds in return.

Every single one of us has our own unique perspective on the world, and that's what makes us special. Our perception is shaped by our self-awareness. Sometimes, without even realising it, we assume that others will behave like us and hold ourselves to the same standards. It's only natural that we tend to attract people who are similar to us. It just makes sense, doesn't it?

You know, it's quite clear when we have great relationships with others because we all like to consider ourselves as good people. However, what may not be so obvious is that the things we dislike about other people often reflect the qualities we don't appreciate in ourselves. Now, although you can't control who you meet in life, you certainly have a choice in deciding whether you want them to remain in your life.

If you constantly find yourself surrounded by negative people who bring you down, it's worth taking a moment to self-reflect:

- ***Do you respect and value yourself?***
- ***Do you truly believe you deserve love and happiness?***

If the answer is "no" to any of these questions, it could be the underlying reason behind this pattern. It is important to surround yourself with people who bring you up, not people who bring you down. And that applies doubly to your relationships. It's important to realise that the people we attract into our lives can offer valuable insights into our own journey of self-discovery and personal growth.

For example, if you play lots of video games you will find that over time you tend to become surrounded by friends who play lots of videogames. If you play lots of sports you tend to find yourself associating with sporty people. This doesn't just apply to hobbies and sports, but to personality traits too. If you exude a fun-loving, happy persona you tend to find yourself associating with the same type of personality.

The negative people who come into your life are trying to teach you something. They shine a light on areas that need healing or improvement. You see, when people are hurt, they often hurt others as well. Being open to their lessons can help you make positive changes and attract better people into your life. It's important to remember that it's not because you're a terrible person that you attract these bad apples. It could be because you struggle with self-esteem and find it hard to say no, which keeps them around.

Have you ever noticed how people tend to treat you a certain way wherever you go? It's worth taking a moment to think about it: is it them, or is it me? It can be tough (and maybe even a bit painful) to admit our own flaws, but that's the first step towards personal growth and attracting better experiences. Every person we meet gives us a chance to learn something new about ourselves and our personalities. Embrace these encounters as opportunities to identify areas where we can heal, improve certain habits, or work on traits that may make us uncomfortable.

This comes down to a lack of self-love and self-esteem for most people.

"So, how do we change that?"

Well. While it's fine to love someone, it's also important to ensure that the feeling is mutual and that you're not investing your love in someone who doesn't want it. Before you can truly love someone else and have a fulfilling relationship, it's crucial to learn how to love yourself and find happiness on your own. Having a partner to share your day with is wonderful, but being overly desperate for companionship can cause you to settle for less than you deserve – and that's NEVER a good idea.

The bottom line is that your "dream guy" will not come in the form of a work in progress. You need to like him just as he is and not think, "Well, if I can change certain things about him, that will be great." No, no, no! You don't have time to fix other people... Plus, it never works! Just think how hard it is to change certain things about yourself, even when you are fully on board with wanting that change. If you think that is hard, imagine how hard it is to change somebody else when they may not even want that change. It's going to be next to impossible.

So, how can you increase your chances of meeting that dream guy?

CHAPTER
14

"Raising your odds".

ou have to be willing to seize any opportunities that come knocking. That's how, in my humble opinion, you'll find your dream guy!

Someone once told me, "Just do what makes you happy, and love will find its way to you." But let me tell you about my old neighbour. By day, he was a care home manager, but by night, he was a PlayStation fiend. We had a heart-to-heart one day about his love life, and he admitted to feeling lonely and wanting to find someone special. However, he couldn't be bothered to try. I genuinely hope he has found his match by now, but I wouldn't bet on it!

"So, how do you know all of this?"

Well, when it comes to relationships and love, we all know it's not solely about luck and good timing. While those factors do play a role, there's much more to it than that. When it comes to men and dating, one thing is crystal clear: you need to put in effort and be prepared both mentally and emotionally. But you know what? Investing time in yourself is worth it and can bring you immense happiness. Man or no man, it might just be one of the best things you'll ever do!

You might be thinking, "Why should I bother putting in so much effort when it seems like men are the ones with commitment issues that are stopping me from having the relationship I want?" Well, in my opinion, people can be divided into two groups: those who love blaming others (the victim mentality) and those who take ownership of their actions and live life on their own terms.

Want to know who is usually happier and more successful at achieving their goals? Well, I'll give you a little clue: it's not the victims!

If you want to live a fantastic life, it's essential to maintain a cheerful outlook when it comes to creating better situations. Remember, it's all about taking realistic actions! Don't get caught up in the desire for instant success. It's important to realise that success doesn't happen overnight. Instead, put your energy into enjoying self-improvement. Remember, good things take time and effort, so be patient and focus on the journey rather than just obsessing over the end result.

"But I never seem to meet any guys. How can I change this?"

Well, let me ask you this: In a typical week, how many men do you usually have real social interactions with? I'm talking about connecting with guys, having proper conversations where you look each other in the eye, and maybe even having a chat that lasts for more than 10-15 minutes. If you're not meeting loads of new guys, it's going to feel like forever before you find your dream guy. I mean, if you're only chatting with one guy a week, the odds aren't exactly in your favour, honey! It can be so frustrating because these interactions are probably just happening by chance, and you don't really get to pick these guys yourself.

It is not rocket science to work out that the more guys you meet, the higher your chances of finding one who really gets you. If you're looking for love, being open to new dating opportunities is crucial. Let's be real: sitting around and waiting for fate to work its magic isn't the most reliable plan!

When you're out there dating, having an abundance mindset totally transforms the whole experience. It's all about being open to endless possibilities and meeting loads of fascinating guys, each with their own incredible stories and outlook on life. So, why limit yourself when there are heaps of potential matches waiting for you? Even if your soulmate doesn't show up right away, every date is a chance to learn more about yourself and figure out what you truly want in a partner.

But here's the thing: if you simply sit around, waiting for your perfect match to miraculously appear at your doorstep, you could potentially miss out on numerous other wonderful opportunities. Moreover, even when that special someone does come along, you might not be adequately prepared to handle it due to a lack of experience. It's akin to going into a job interview for your dream job without any prior preparation – no practice or readiness. In such a scenario, you would likely stumble over your words, overlook crucial cues, and, unfortunately, wrecking your chances of securing that perfect job.

It's important to gain some dating experience, even if it means enduring a few less-than-stellar dates. Believe it or not, these experiences can teach you valuable life skills such as effective communication, empathy, and handling rejection with grace. So, don't be too discouraged if the dating scene isn't always easy! These experiences also help you understand your preferences in a partner and identify qualities that are important to you. By actively seeking new experiences, you increase your chances of finding the right person and growing as an individual.

Just be yourself and let your true beauty shine through. The right person will recognise and admire the unique qualities that make you beautiful. Don't let anyone dictate your worth based on some silly Instagram trend. You are more than enough just the way you are. Remember, real beauty comes from within.

You might be the sweetest nectarine out there, but hey, not everyone is a fan of nectarines! So, if someone doesn't appreciate you, don't worry about it. It's their loss, and it says more about them than it does about you. Keep shining!

"So, how do I meet more guys?"

This is it.

Unless you're hosting a party and your mate brings a new face, the chances of bumping into your one true love in your living room are slim. If you're lounging in front of the telly in your ketchup-stained hoody all day, it's highly unlikely that Prince Charming will suddenly show up at your door.

If you're all about living your best life, being happy in your bubble, doing awesome and thrilling things just for yourself, and being where the action is with a friendly and open attitude, then trust me, people will start paying attention to you.

Before you go and meet your dream guy, let me share a secret with you: In life, all kinds of people simply sit around and wait for things to happen. They patiently wait for the perfect moment to start a conversation or hope that someone else will make the first move. They rely on others to show enough interest so they can avoid rejection. They're constantly waiting for an invitation and the confidence to act. Don't be like them! Take charge and go after what you want!

Let's face it: life is constantly telling us to be patient and wait for what we want. But honestly, waiting often leads to either getting something totally off track or just plain nothing. So, here's a couple of questions for you to ponder:

1. *Am I just chilling here, waiting for life to happen, or am I out there being proactive and making things happen?*
2. *What's the deal with my love life? Will all the effort I'm putting in pay off in the end?*

No matter where you are, remember that you have choices. You can either relax and wait for things to unfold or take control and make things happen on your own terms. It's completely up to you.

"Why can't I find a decent guy? Do they even exist?

Alright, I may not possess any superpowers like x-ray vision or mind-reading, but trust me, I've had countless conversations with women. And let me tell you, some complaints about men are just plain silly. I've heard it all and used to believe the same things myself if I am honest. However, here's the truth – these beliefs aren't beneficial to anyone, and they only hinder your progress. It's time to debunk these myths once and for all!

Have you ever heard yourself telling your bestie:

"There are no decent guys out there."

"Decent guys are looking for someone who is hotter and prettier than me."

"Men are not interested in someone like me."

"Men aren't really into commitment or relationships. They just want casual hook-ups."

If you have these misconceptions, then stop it! These statements are absolute nonsense and can ruin your chances of finding love. It's time to forget about them and start fresh in the dating scene.

We've all experienced the ups and downs of love and heartbreak, and wow, can it leave a lasting impact! These challenging experiences can make it difficult to move forward, but here's the thing: if we allow them to dictate our future relationships, where will that lead us? It's important to remember that not everyone is the same. So, let's not judge potential partners based on past experiences. We deserve to find the love we desire without being hindered by what others have done to us in the past!

Here is a question, though … What do you want in a partner? … Let's get into it:

CHAPTER

15

"Working out what you want".

*A*lright, let's dive into it... It is crucial to be honest about your desires when it comes to finding a future partner. It will be difficult to find happiness in your love life if you are unsure about what you want or the reasons behind those desires. Being truthful to yourself about your wants is a key factor in attracting the right person for a meaningful relationship.

So, what are your big life goals? Are you dreaming of a successful and fulfilling career? Or perhaps starting a family and enjoying the suburban dream in a beautiful house? Or is jetting off on thrilling adventures more your style?

Finding a partner who shares the same desires becomes much simpler once you figure out what you truly want. It's also great because knowing your life goals helps you recognise the qualities you'd love to see in your ideal match. For instance, if starting a family is important to you, it's wise to seek someone who is dependable, loving, and adores kids. And if exploring the world is your passion, finding an adventurous and spontaneous partner would be a perfect fit!

"I am struggling to think about the traits I want in a partner. How do I do this?"

Well, start by thinking about the things you value in other people in your life, such as:
- *Are there any traits that your friends have that you love?*
- *Are there any traits that your friends have that you hate?*

Add those to your list: consider the characteristics you need in a partner, the ones you want, and the ones that aren't necessary but would be nice to have. Remember, there is no such thing as the perfect partner! Let me share a story with you: one of my clients had only one item on her list - "The police don't have a warrant out for his arrest" – we had a good chat about that, I can assure you!

Now, let's take a moment to reflect on ourselves and our personality traits and consider how well they would complement others.

- *What is your religious/political beliefs? It's worth finding someone who shares your beliefs. It's always nice to have someone who understands your perspective and can engage in meaningful discussions about the subjects you're passionate about.*
- *Are you a fan of hitting the gym and eating healthy? You might struggle with a partner who isn't into it or prefers to laze on the couch, watch Netflix, and eat chocolate.*
- *What about temperature preferences? If someone feels cold when it's 79°F, they might find it tough to live with you if you like the windows open in winter.*
- *Do you love a good adrenaline rush? It can be really frustrating to deal with someone who gets their thrills from simply watching TV.*
- *Do you prefer to save money and be financially responsible? Dealing with someone who constantly splurges on impulse purchases can be quite annoying.*

Take a moment to reflect on your past relationships. Did you notice anything that you genuinely appreciated in one partner but weren't so fond of in others? It's possible that there were certain traits that you simply couldn't imagine living with or without.

But listen, it's important not to base your list of partner criteria solely on previous relationships that turned out badly.

Doing so can lead you to choose a partner who is also not a good fit for you. Why? Well, if we create a list based on past failures and our own trauma, someone might meet every single point on that list but still not be a genuinely good person. Having standards is important, but they should be based on an emotionally healthy perspective and our own needs rather than creating a checklist for a partner.

Years ago, I went through a tough breakup. My ex would lose control, shouting and screaming when angry, which I couldn't tolerate. When I entered my next relationship, my new boyfriend had a different way of dealing with anger – he would go silent and disappear for days whenever he was upset. In my mind, I thought the silent treatment was preferable to the shouting, but I soon realised how wrong I was! It turned out that it was equally damaging in its own way.

In the long run, shared values and decent behaviour are much more important in a relationship. It's easy to find people with exciting interests and good looks, but they may also be high-maintenance or selfish.

Before you head out and start chasing your dream guy, it's crucial to clearly understand what you're aiming for. And you MUST be picky, and I will explain why...

CHAPTER

16

"Being selective is the key".

*H*ey, remember that amazing dream guy you were manifesting with your list earlier? Well, let's transform that fantasy into a concrete plan to make it happen!

As I have already said, being selective is the key to success when it comes to love. I always say to give someone your trust until they prove they can't be trusted. Trust and giving people the benefit of the doubt is important, but it's also crucial to be discerning. Look out for signs that they are trustworthy before fully investing in them. It's always wise to keep your eyes wide open!

"What does being selective mean?"

Well, it means holding out for a guy who possesses the qualities you deem most important – someone who brings you more happiness than sadness and supports and enhances your life just by being present. For example, 'Is it your dream to get a degree or write a book? Does he wholeheartedly support and encourage you in that, or does he roll his eyes? This man may occasionally hurt, disappoint, or even anger you because he is human, and humans are prone to such behaviours. While setting high standards is important, it's also crucial to be realistic. Aim for an exceptional man (in your eyes) but remember that perfection doesn't exist in humans.

Let me return to the question I have previously asked: Whom do you want to attract into your life, and what kind of person do you want to be?

I get it; asking this question can be tough. But it's important to understand yourself and strive to become the person you aspire to be. This is crucial if you want to attract the right people into your life. It's not uncommon for us to end up with Mr. Wrong or even a few Mr. Wrongs before realising we deserve better. Sometimes, it takes experiencing multiple failures, heartbreaks, emotional distress, and pain for us to finally reach this conclusion.

If you are upfront and honest with yourself about your true desires from the beginning, you can avoid getting involved with the wrong guy (or guys). Often, it's because of your own personal issues and concerns, such as fear of being alone or running out of time. Does that sound familiar?

Settling for any guy who shows interest can be a self-sabotaging pattern. Sometimes, we tend to overlook flaws in guys we have a strong bond with and start imagining them as amazing, even if that might not be the case. It's like we lose our ability to see things objectively and forget that we have other options.

Listen, I know it's not easy to find a man with whom you have incredible chemistry. But that doesn't mean we should turn a blind eye to the flaws of the men we're dating just because we have great sexual chemistry (that wears off fast, let me tell you). We often set high expectations for men because we have dreams and desires, too. You know, relationships can sometimes go from 0 to 100 really fast, and suddenly, people start expecting commitment right off the bat.

I need to hammer this home, honey. It's SO important to be super selective regarding potential relationships. I cannot impress this on you enough. By being pickier, we have a higher chance of finding the RIGHT partner at the right time. Be strong and make smart decisions. Don't be afraid to say "no" if a guy doesn't meet your standards. Setting high expectations right from the start of your dating adventure is crucial. Know what you want, and don't settle for anything less!

I've said this before, and I'll repeat it: admiration plays a significant role in attraction and love. So, let me ask you a question: When you meet a new guy, take a moment to reflect. Do you genuinely admire who he is as a person?

I mean, when he talks about topics like work, family, friends, hobbies, or ambitions – things that aren't directly about you. Do you find yourself thinking, "Wow! This guy is truly kind-hearted, intelligent, creative, and hard-working"? Do you trust their opinion and knowledge?

Take a moment to ask yourself if he is someone you would genuinely enjoy spending time with and potentially becoming best friends with. Imagine looking at your relationship from an outsider's perspective – would it appear healthy and happy?

Would you be happy seeing your loved one (mom, aunt, sister, best friend, or daughter) in a relationship with someone just like him? It's important to consider how he treats you, gives you attention, and interacts with others. How does he treat his siblings, parents, friends, or even strangers like restaurant waiters? Observing these interactions lets you determine if he is the right fit for you.

One day, when I was around 23 years old, I remember my friend saying, "You know what, Kel? You're a big jar, but you see yourself as a small one." I didn't quite understand what she meant, but I felt deep down that it was a compliment. I just nodded and smiled at her.

Years later (yes, *years)*, her words rang in my ears. They resonated with me deeply when I experienced the loss of my beautiful, amazing mum, Hilda, and it was then that I realised I had spent my whole life settling for less. I had been thinking small and living a mediocre life.

My jobs, my relationships … everything was good enough, but nothing was great. I hadn't been prioritising myself or appreciating the present moment. I hadn't been utilising my talents or making the most of my gifts. I wasn't even aware of what my talents were. I had forgotten that we only have one life, and I certainly wasn't living mine to the fullest.

I came to realise, much later in life, that I've placed far too much importance on what others thought of me. I've spent an excessive amount of time trying to please everyone around me without considering what is truly right for ME and putting my own needs first. It always felt like it was selfish to prioritise myself, but now I see the absolute importance of self-care and setting firm boundaries. It is not selfish – in fact, it is utterly necessary.

Then, one day, it dawned on me that the opinions and thoughts of those I was so concerned about were irrelevant. Their opinion of me was none of my business! It was a real revelation; I can tell you. That day, it hit me that what truly mattered was how I perceived myself. Please repeat after me: Prioritising yourself is NOT selfish; in fact, it is one of the most crucial acts of self-care you can undertake.

The thing is, once you realise the importance of self-care and self-love, you also realise the significance of taking the time to reflect on the kind of guy who can enhance your life and make you feel safe and secure. It's one of the most important things you can do my darling. It's not about being egotistical, selfish, or self-centred, but rather recognising that we only have one short life. This exact realisation was why I felt compelled to write this book. It would all be worth it if I can help just one person out there. Pursuing what we truly want gives us the best chance to experience happiness and live an amazing, fulfilling life. Can you even imagine that?

I have been guilty of entering jobs, relationships and friendships that did not serve me well. Deep down, I probably felt that I didn't deserve anything better. However, all it did was bring me a lifetime of feeling inadequate and allowing others to mistreat me.

I have finally accepted that I am the captain of my own ship and that I should prioritise myself. As a result, I have noticed my jar of happiness and fulfilment growing bigger and bigger. Now, I am truly in love with my life – one that is filled with hope, excitement, and endless possibilities.

And now, I would like to take a moment to sit down and tell you, the amazing woman reading this, that you are also a big jar. I just hope it doesn't take you as long to realise it as it took me.

Anyway, on another note, let's dive into this crucial topic...

CHAPTER
17

"Keep your eyes wide open".

Since we were young, we've been taught to be nice and avoid hurting anyone's feelings at all costs. But let me be real with you – honesty is seriously important, especially when it comes to dating. Just be true to yourself, speak your mind confidently, and don't hold back from expressing how you feel. Knowing what you want and communicating it boldly to your partner is perfectly fine. If a guy isn't living up to your expectations, go ahead and tell him directly.

"But won't that put him off?"

No way!

Being honest can make you even more appealing to the right guy. Men appreciate open and upfront women about themselves and their relationship goals. Knowing how you feel and where you stand in the relationship gives them confidence, and it can bring you closer together.

We must remember that guys can't read our minds (even though it would be great if they could), so it's important to communicate openly with them about what we're thinking and what we need to make us happy.

If you want to make a real impact with a guy, being upfront and honest about your expectations from the start is important. Being open about what you want will set the tone for the relationship. This kind of honesty can help you achieve your goals by subtly conveying that you're in control.

You can't simply pretend to be happy and expect everything to fall into place magically. It's important to genuinely feel happiness and believe in yourself to achieve your goals. Rather than forcing things, it's best to let them unfold naturally. Practice patience and make wise decisions when building meaningful relationships that will bring you long-term benefits.

Let's talk about the six-six-six guys…

Six Foot

Six Figures

Six Pack

There's a ton of guys out there who are really into the online dating game, and why not? They've got girls falling at their feet. But these lads aren't looking to put a ring on it anytime soon. While other guys might be up for dating just about anyone, these men think highly of themselves and wouldn't dream of going out with someone unless they've been scouted for Victoria's Secret!

These fellas, let's call them the "Triple Six Squad," have a world of gorgeous women at their fingertips, just a mouse click away. They're all about having fun and living in the moment. Their dating styles are totally laid-back—no rigid plans here!

They're not on a mad dash to find 'The One'. And if they stumble upon a date, that's more disaster than delight? No biggie! They don't waste time moping around or over-analysing it. Instead, they dust themselves off with a shrug and stride forward into the next girl without missing a beat.

I think men have a slight advantage when it comes to committed relationships. Women often could approach any man they're interested in and have a good chance of getting him into bed. However, from that point onward, the power dynamic shifts.

On the other hand, men generally have more control over deciding how exclusive they want to be in a relationship.

I remember a phrase that seems to hold true:

"Women sleep with who they want, men sleep with who they can... but men marry who they want, and women marry who they can."

You may have noticed already that sometimes, you come across guys who let their looks and skills go to their head and use dating solely to boost their ego. You know, those guys who are completely full of themselves and love flaunting their skills to attract women?

Well, it's quite common to come across this kind of behaviour in guys who maybe didn't receive much attention from the ladies when they were younger or struggled with self-esteem issues. However, as they have become more physically fit, financially well-off, or influential, things have drastically changed for them.

It's important to note that some of these guys may still have unresolved issues with women and view dating as an opportunity to seek revenge on those who have rejected them in the past. As a result, they may tend to treat their "conquests" poorly.

Men of this type are naturally inclined towards physical attractiveness rather than emotional bonds. As mentioned before, they often prioritise quantity over quality in their relationships. They believe that there are plenty of amazing women out there, and given the perfect opportunity, they believe they could potentially date any one of them.

In my coaching sessions, I have made a truly fascinating observation. Nowadays, many men seem to prefer to keep their options open and date multiple women before committing to a serious relationship. By getting to know different women, they can figure out their preferences in a partner. On the flip side, women still tend to focus on one guy at a time when it comes to dating.

"So, how can I find the right balance, then?"

Ok ... Have you ever encountered those women who always appear to be in relationships, as if being single is too uncomfortable for them? It can feel like being single makes them feel like a loser in terms of love ...

But you know what's interesting? Sometimes, constantly being in relationships can be a way for some people to avoid facing themselves or dealing with their own emotions. It's like using the distraction of a relationship to escape from personal growth or self-reflection.

Being single can bring up uncomfortable feelings for some people. It might make them confront things they've been avoiding or make them feel vulnerable in a way that being with someone else doesn't.

But here's the thing – embracing those uncomfortable moments and truly getting to know yourself during periods of being single can lead to healthier and more fulfilling relationships in the future. It's all about balancing enjoying your company and sharing your life with someone else when the time is right.

It's important to remember that taking breaks between relationships is okay. Use that time to focus on yourself and figure out what you truly want and need from a partner. After all, the most important relationship you'll ever have is the one you have with yourself!

On the flip side, some women choose to remain single and avoid dating altogether. They say they are very happy being single and are not on the lookout for a relationship.

And you know what? That's perfectly okay too! Some women find fulfilment and happiness in focusing on themselves, their careers, friendships, hobbies, or personal growth without the need for a romantic relationship.

Choosing to be single doesn't mean you're missing out on anything. In fact, it's a bold decision that shows strength and independence. You have the power to create your own happiness and define what love means to you. It's horses for courses.

Whether you're happily single or open to the idea of a relationship in the future, it's all about embracing who you are and living life on your own terms.

However, it can be far more challenging for women who constantly jump from one relationship to another or for those who fear dating.

Dating plays a vital role in helping you develop essential skills for spotting a healthy relationship. It's not just about finding a great guy; it's also about learning how to spot the duds and understanding what you truly want in a partner.

Additionally, it helps improve personal communication skills and the ability to interpret body language. So, if you are always in serious relationships one after another, or if you're someone who refuses to date at all, it's going to be quite difficult to spot somebody who could potentially be perfect for you.

CHAPTER
18

"The C Word"

his is a dicey topic, but let's address it head-on. Many women ask me what it takes for a man to commit to her.

However, before you set your expectations on commitment from a guy, it's crucial to understand its true meaning. Let me share some insights with you about commitment, relationships, and men. Here's the truth—men don't commit solely because a woman expresses her desire for something serious. It takes more than that for them to commit fully.

Just take a moment to consider this: Having a long-lasting, healthy, and satisfying relationship is important for everyone, regardless of gender. Now, let's address a common misconception that some women may have. There is this notion that they need to have "the talk" with men to make the relationship official.

Wrong!!!

While discussing commitment is important in a relationship, true commitment has nothing to do with just the conversations and words exchanged between a man and a woman. It's all about actions and genuine dedication! When it comes to commitment, it's important to understand that it's not a casual conversation. For men, it goes much deeper. It's a mix of various factors that resonate within them. No amount of talking can truly capture the strength and significance of this heartfelt decision.

It's unfortunate, but many women don't approach situations with men in this way. Instead, they tend to cling to preconceived notions of how relationships with men should be. By not embracing their own situation's uniqueness, they often wonder why things don't turn out as expected. Don't waste your time trying to change yourself to meet someone else's expectations.

Instead, concentrate on finding someone who is right for YOU. And believe me, experience counts in the dating game. The more you date, the more you'll learn about yourself and what you truly want in a partner. It also helps you avoid repeating past mistakes.

When you believe that your partner owes you a perfect relationship, you're setting yourself up for a big disappointment. When a woman desires a picture-perfect relationship, like the ones portrayed in romantic books and films, she is setting herself up for disappointment. It becomes more about chasing an idealistic vision rather than seeing and appreciating the real person right in front of her. So, as I have already said, never 'settle,' but also, you need to not rely solely on a man to make you happy. You must find that happiness within yourself.

When you're unsure about the direction of your relationship, there are some clear signs to watch out for. One common mistake is assuming that just because you and your partner are close, they automatically share all your dreams and aspirations. It's important to remember that even in the closest relationships, each person has their own desires and needs. Keeping this in mind is crucial.

As women, we all have desires and needs in relationships, even if we don't always express them openly. It's common for us to keep these expectations to ourselves, maybe because we're unsure how to bring them up or because we're afraid it might overwhelm the guy.

I've come to realise that when a woman doesn't clearly express her thoughts to a man out of fear of "scaring him off" or making him defensive, it can lead to different expectations.

It's crucial for both parties to communicate openly and honestly to avoid any misunderstandings. To prevent conflicts or misunderstandings, it's essential to be completely upfront and honest in your communication.

"But why is being upfront about what I want so important?"

Being upfront about what you want is crucial for healthy and fulfilling relationships; when you clearly communicate your desires and expectations, you set the foundation for open and honest communication, which is essential for healthy relationships. This helps both you and your partner understand each other's needs and work towards meeting them.

Being upfront allows you to avoid future misunderstandings, resentment, and disappointment. It's all about building trust and creating a strong connection that is rooted in mutual understanding and respect. By communicating openly from the start, you set the foundation for a healthier and more fulfilling relationship.

To be clear, assuming things and committing before he does can put unnecessary pressure, anxiety, and tension on the relationship. So, it's best to take it easy and not rush things. We are sometimes guilty of secretly hoping that a guy will have a change of heart and be open to settling down, even if he keeps saying he's not ready or not interested.

We convince ourselves that our deep connection will eventually make him unable to resist wanting a relationship with us. Have you ever found yourself in this situation? If so, how did it turn out?

It's a common mistake to find ourselves taking the lead in a relationship and hoping that our partner will know exactly what we want from him and step up and be the perfect boyfriend or husband. We let our imaginations run riot and have high expectations, even when he's showing clear signs that he doesn't feel the same way.

But let me tell you, this is a big boo-boo because then, when things don't go exactly as we meticulously planned in our heads, we tend to get grumpy and moody. It can be confusing for a man when he finds himself in this situation, not knowing what he has done wrong.

All he sees is that we have suddenly become an emotional wreck and seem extremely disappointed. And guess who gets all the blame? Yup, you guessed it - him!

Behaving in this way won't exactly help you get closer to him. I know there might be some people who disagree, but trust me, I've seen many women end up feeling miserable and fed up with it. Approaching issues in a way which doesn't make him feel like you are 'blaming' him is key. By being more honest about your desires and worrying less about immediate outcomes, you'll gain a clearer understanding of your situation.

As a result, your short-term expectations and outlook will change, leading to a more enjoyable experience and a higher chance of finding happiness in your love life.

Whenever I witness a woman trying to convince a man to do something through persuasion, manipulation, or pressure, especially if the man seems hesitant or unsure, it just feels like trouble waiting to happen. You are never going to change what a man thinks, believes, or feels, and trying to will only ever cause problems, but you can let him know what YOU think, believe, and feel.

When I see women resorting to tactics like whining, begging, or throwing tantrums to get their way, they may not realise that it can harm their credibility in relationships. It's important to find more effective ways of communicating and compromising instead. It's not about you stamping your foot and insisting on 'winning' an exchange and, by default, him having to 'lose', but rather achieving the compromise where both sides win, or at least neither is forced to feel like they lose and both of you feel heard.

So, on that note, what is the best way forward?

CHAPTER
19

"The persuading game"

o, when you're upfront and honest about what you want, you take the risk that some guys will run for the hills. But honestly, isn't that a blessing?

If you're clear about your desires and communicate them to a guy, he'll either step up or step out. It's as simple as that. Just stay focused on what you truly want and don't be afraid to let go of Mr. Wrong because, in the end, the more time you are with Mr. Wrong the less you are looking for Mr Right. Ultimately, it's a win-win situation!

If you find yourself trying to force a connection with a guy you're interested in, but it feels like you're not "clicking" or understanding each other, then it probably won't work out.

Either he gets you, or he doesn't. But don't let that discourage you from working on yourself and growing every day. It just means that if he can't appreciate your journey, he is 100% not the right match for you. The trick is to NOT fear scaring a guy off … See it as the trash putting itself out.

When you're with the right guy, conversations flow effortlessly, and you both understand each other's desires. There's no pressure to constantly come up with something interesting to say just to keep him interested. He genuinely wants to stick around, and the connection speaks for itself. You don't have to worry about being a bother to him either, because it's obvious that he enjoys spending time with you.

When you meet the right guy, it's like magic. You'll feel it in your gut, and everything will just fall into place, and you will not question his intentions. The connection will be so genuine and natural that it's impossible to resist and it will just feel right!

On the flip side, no matter how much effort you put in with the wrong guy, that authentic connection will always be out of reach. You'll know it when you find yourself talking to your friends and family, and googling reasons for why you feel so anxious about him.

In a healthy relationship (the ONLY type you should want), it's crucial to have open discussions about differences, find a compromise during disagreements, and navigate conflicts together. It's not solely about finding the perfect match or expecting everything to be magical and perfect 100% of the time as that is not realistic, life is full of ups and downs. The importance lays in how the ups and downs are dealt with.

When two people's intentions and desires match up, it never scares the right guy off, it only strengthens the trust and connection between you. As I have already said, you can't force a man to be who you want him to be, just like a man shouldn't expect you to hide your emotions.

If you try too hard to make a guy commit, he might start feeling overwhelmed and pull away. This can lead to various problems, and ultimately, the relationship may not work out. So, it's best to go with the flow and avoid pushing things too much. When faced with resistance, some women may unknowingly resort to pressuring.

When it comes to a man, it's important to pay attention to his actions. If he isn't trying to discuss the future, showing genuine interest in your thoughts and desires, or inquiring about your loved ones, it may be a cause for concern.

This type of indirect communication may suggest that he might not genuinely be interested in a future with you.

When you've spent a significant amount of time with a guy, you can typically gauge his level of comfort around you through his words, actions, or even his silence. These cues can be quite telling and provide you with insight into how he perceives you and your relationship.

Navigating through differences in desires or preferences between you and a guy can be quite challenging, right? You might think that arguing or trying to convince him would change his feelings or wants, but it usually doesn't work out that way. Instead, wouldn't it be better to understand and accept each other's viewpoints as a step towards finding common ground?

When you try to persuade him, he might resist – it's just how we humans are wired. We tend not to easily give in to what others want from us. So, when this happens, don't let it throw you off balance; remember, it's just a typical human response!

I mean, have you ever been approached by someone who starts friendly and flattering, making you think it's just a casual chat? But then, suddenly, you get that gut feeling that something isn't quite right. It's like a light bulb moment that reveals the true reality of the situation.

And then it hits you…

"This person is just trying to convince me to do something that benefits THEM."

Boom! Out of left field, the conversation takes a sudden turn, completely shifting your perspective on the chat and the person you're interacting with. Suddenly, you start to pick up on the deeper meaning behind their compliments, tone of voice, and mannerisms like never before. It becomes clear that their persuasive tactics are quite evident, almost as if they are intentionally trying to manipulate and influence you. This can instantly create feelings of discomfort and tension.

When your mind or body feels pressured by external sources. It naturally responds with resistance. It is important to note that this applies to both men and women, as both genders react similarly when faced with persuasion.

What's more, turning the persuasion dial up too high or resorting to pleading can boomerang right back at you, causing more harm than good. And this is particularly true for guys. Acting this way doesn't just colour his current viewpoint but also shapes how they see you and the entire relationship.

As we get older, if we're fortunate, we come to realise that this approach no longer serves us. We become wise enough to let go of this behaviour when it comes to most of the people in our lives. We come to accept that it is not our place to change them, not our place to convince them that we are right. We can say our piece and we can let them say theirs, and we can agree or disagree, and that's OK.

But here's the thing: When our emotions are running wild in our love lives, we tend to fall back into our old habits. When faced with a crisis, it's common for all of us to react impulsively and behave in ways that we may not be proud of. Similarly, it's easy to unintentionally undermine your credibility when trying to persuade someone, especially men. (Stay with me, alright?)

When you engage in convincing behaviours, you might unintentionally show that you rely emotionally on a man's decisions and actions, which can result in giving up some control. It's crucial to approach relationships with a balanced mindset.

While it's normal to invest time and emotions in someone you care about, it's equally important to make sure your efforts are reciprocated. Going all-in from the beginning and prioritising his needs without receiving the same level of dedication in return may not be the most beneficial approach for your emotional well-being.

If he hasn't earned it, he won't appreciate it—or you. *Remember, men value the things they've worked for.*

Hey, this concept isn't just for guys. Let's look at it from a different angle…

Picture this: You're on a first date, and the guy surprises you with a 10-carat diamond necklace. Sounds great in theory, doesn't it? But if that really did happen, you might not be too thrilled or grateful. Instead, it could make you feel kind of weirded out and suspicious—like they were trying to buy your affection or had some ulterior motive. It would be too much, too soon … simply too weird!

Even if you liked it, enjoying that gift would be difficult because the whole situation would feel over-the-top and rushed and would make you question his intention.

If a man tries to monopolise your time, devotion, and sexual attention too quickly, it can lead to an uncomfortable situation, instead of the wonderful experience it should be. Maybe he imagines himself playing a significant role in your future, but he should earn that place instead of demanding it.

I've mentioned this before, but it's worth repeating. It's another factor that contributes to a guy's underlying insecurity: he wants to believe that he is the ONLY person who could have won you over. He doesn't want to think that any random guy who took you out for a few dinners and movies could have captured your attention as well.

Let's say you've just met someone, and within a few weeks, they're already declaring their eternal love for you. That's a major red flag … with flashing lights!

It's not uncommon for people who have experienced trauma or have abandonment issues to fall into this trap. It may take years for you to finally realise that their love wasn't genuine at all. They weren't head over heels for you, they were just desperate to be with anyone because being alone was too much for them to handle.

Even if you're not putting in much effort to win a guy over, deep down he'll sense your fear and desperation. It's like this hidden energy that's driving you.

So, how do you find the balance?

CHAPTER
20

"Don't rush it".

*F*inding balance in relationships, especially in dating, is imperative. It's crucial to find the right level of give and take.

Typically, there is a cycle of commitment where one person may be more invested than the other. It's all about finding that sweet spot. Most relationships tend to follow a somewhat predictable pattern. This concept revolves around the belief that love and desire are delicately balanced and can be easily disrupted by common behaviours exhibited by both men and women.

I've noticed an interesting dynamic in which women often try to convince a man they are the right match for him. However, this can sometimes create an imbalance in the relationship dynamics. Now, I'm not here to tell you what to do, but I want to have a real talk with you about what guys are thinking.

Here's a truth bomb: If your goal is to get married, setting up home with a guy before marriage might not be the wisest idea!

It must be said that I am in no way against living together outside of marriage. You need to realise your long-term goals and work towards them.

Regarding relationships, guys must be committed and willing to make sacrifices to thrive. Men must recognise that a successful relationship requires effort and dedication. If they are unwilling to invest in finance, social connections, or emotions, they might bail as soon as things get tough.

When a married man faces issues in his relationship, he often feels a stronger motivation to resolve them. The public commitment and social consequences of failure push him to work things out. However, sometimes, there may not be enough external pressure to encourage him to act.

We shouldn't forget the differences in how men and women view moving in together. Many guys see cohabitation as a trial run for marriage or simply enjoying the perks without committing to a lifelong partnership. On the other hand, women often see moving in with a man as a step towards something more serious and long-term (which is not necessarily reality!).

While moving in together may seem like a natural step towards marriage, it can sometimes exacerbate issues instead of resolving them. Choosing to live together without getting married can amplify relationship problems. When you're simply cohabiting, it becomes easier for one partner to end the relationship and just walk away if they become bored, lose interest, or reach their breaking point.

Jumping into cohabiting too quickly without careful consideration can lead to problems later. That's why taking time and thinking before diving in headfirst is important.

We all understand the significance of compatibility in a relationship. You can determine if you're a good match by getting to know someone and assessing whether you share similar values, interests, and goals. Rushing into a relationship without proper thought may result in future issues if you're incompatible.

So, in simple terms, you need to be mindful of a few things when it comes to relationships. It's important to think things through and ensure compatibility with the other person.

You also want to invest emotionally and grow together. If things get too intense too quickly, take a step back, take it easy and let things progress naturally. Many men don't appreciate what they have if it's handed to them on a silver platter – they need a little challenge!

Don't you just hate it when you see this same emotional pattern playing out repeatedly? It feels like a never-ending cycle with no end in sight.

Have you ever been through this with a guy? Don't worry, you're not alone. It's common for us ladies to go through this kind of thing. Isn't it ironic how the more you try to talk about your feelings and be open, the more he pulls away and shuts down? Ugh, it's so frustrating!

So, here's the deal when it comes to relationships. Suppose you dive in headfirst and start bending over backwards for your partner right from the start, rearranging your schedule, providing emotional support without expecting anything in return, without them putting in any effort. In that case, they might not appreciate it or you. Men generally appreciate something more when they've worked for it. READ THAT AGAIN!

It's understandable to feel frustrated and upset when a guy keeps avoiding you and showing no interest. It can affect you and make it harder to deal with the situation. Remember, constantly begging or pressuring him for commitment will only push him away faster. Being overly needy and emotional all the time is a big turn-off. Stay independent and let things develop naturally.

As I have already said, if you're constantly being too pushy and trying to convince a guy about this or that, believe it or not, it might blow up in your face and ruin your chances with him. It may seem counterintuitive, but being overly persuasive increases the likelihood of him losing interest and attraction to you.

Think of it this way …

Have you ever had a guy who desperately tried to convince you to date or be in a relationship with him, even though it was clear that you weren't interested? And if you didn't respond positively, did he ramp up his efforts even more? I bet if he did that, you wouldn't suddenly be taken with him because of his needy actions and pleadings. Would you be? You were probably repelled by everything he did instead of becoming more attracted to him.

Men can often feel clueless when it comes to dating and relationships. Understanding and expressing emotions and intimacy can be particularly challenging for them, much more so than for us. At the start of a relationship, many men may be unaware of women's expectations, while many women assume that men should already know what seems obvious to them as women.

Not all guys view sex as a sign of being in a serious or exclusive relationship. Some may prefer to have multiple partners and keep their options open. It may sound a bit inappropriate, but it's important to note that men don't hold these views simply because they're "players" or "sex-crazed". While that may be the case in some instances, there is often something deeper happening with most men. Let me explain.

CHAPTER

21

"I don't want anything serious".

*I*t's not surprising that men often have a natural inclination towards casual dating, as they tend to be less particular and have multiple sexual partners. This can be attributed to their inherent nature, which explains why they often seek quantity in certain areas. It's simply a part of their DNA. Humans have their fair share of biological instincts, just like any other species. However, what sets us apart is our incredible ability to make conscious choices and decisions.

I need to point out that not all guys are solely interested in racking up numbers when it comes to dating or intimacy. Some are looking for more than just playing a numbers game. Girl, it's your job to spot the difference!

When finding a partner, women typically look for a man with the qualities they desire in a long-term relationship. On the other hand, men may have a biological urge to explore multiple partners. It's like an age-old instinct ingrained in their genes – they have a strong drive to pass on their valuable genes and ensure the continuation of their line.

This is part of why, back in the Middle Ages, it was seen as important that the woman be a virgin, while nobody cared if the man was. This seems to have come through to modern times still in the unfair way that men who have had lots of sexual partners are seen as studs by their peers. At the same time, unfortunately, women with similar histories often do not enjoy such positive reputations.

But trust me, there are plenty of guys out there who genuinely want to form a deep connection with you right from the start. The million-dollar question is... how can you tell if the guy you're dating is looking for a serious partnership with you?

Well, this little list will make it clearer for you. If he's doing the following, then things are looking good:

- **Consistency:** When a guy is head over heels for you and envisions a future together, he will prioritise spending quality time with you. Communication will flow effortlessly, and you can rely on him to consistently show his commitment through both actions and words.

- **Future planning:** If he can't stop talking about the future and includes you in all his plans, it's a sign that he is emotionally available. A guy who is genuinely serious about being in a long-term relationship with you will be open and honest about his emotions. He won't hesitate to share his deepest thoughts, feelings, and dreams. Moreover, he will genuinely listen when you pour your heart out.

- **Shared values and goals:** When you and your partner share the same values and goals, it increases the chances of having a long-lasting relationship and creates a strong foundation for your future together. If he genuinely shows interest in understanding your values and actively seeks common ground, that's a sign that he's serious about building something meaningful with you. It indicates that he's invested in your relationship.

- **Effort and investment:** A guy who is serious about you will go above and beyond! He will invest time, effort, and resources to nurture the relationship. He'll plan special dates, remember those important little details about you, and offer support in every aspect of your life.

- **Commitment to communication:** Establishing a solid foundation in a relationship is crucial. When your partner is willing to have tough conversations, address concerns, and navigate conflicts, it's a sign of their dedication to building a strong future with you!

- **Integration into each other's lives:** When a guy is truly committed to a long-term relationship, he will ensure you become an integral part of his life. And guess what? He'll be just as eager to be a part of your life, too! You can expect to meet his family and friends and enjoy sharing hobbies and activities.

- **Mutual respect and trust:** A man truly committed to a long-term relationship will treat you like royalty. He will show you the utmost respect and trust in your decisions. Not only that, but he will also be your biggest supporter as you strive for personal growth and independence.

This is just a friendly reminder that these signs are not fool proof. It's important to stay vigilant and have honest chats with your partner to ensure you're both on the same page regarding your relationship goals and expectations.

Red flag alert: If you're experiencing intense butterflies, questioning his intentions, feeling unsure or insecure, or seeking advice from friends or family about him, then your gut instinct is kicking in—and you should listen to it! Those butterflies might be your body's way of warning you to be cautious. It's always important to trust your gut instincts regarding relationships.

But let's refocus on how to find the right guy. Because, let's face it, understanding men can sometimes be tricky.

Another thing to watch out for is how a guy introduces you when you're out together and run into one of his acquaintances. Pay close attention to how he introduces you … whether he refers to you as his "friend" or just by your name. It's important not to fool yourself – if that's all he sees you as, then that's the reality. It can be tough to face, but let's be honest: if a guy is unsure about what he wants, chances are he isn't satisfied with what he already has (which is you). As women, we often overlook this principle when we like a guy.

Also, paying attention to his words and, most importantly, his actions is important. As they say, actions speak louder than words, but we must also know that people can be incredibly manipulative. Let me give you an example:

A few years back, I met this cute guy who clarified that he wasn't interested in a relationship. He explained that it wasn't about me but his reasons like work commitments and other factors. However, despite his words, his actions seemed to say otherwise. He would plan and initiate dates, engage in deep conversations, and discuss a future together. It was all so confusing and gave me mixed messages.

Even after I bluntly expressed my lack of interest in a "friends with benefits" situation and made it clear that I wouldn't engage in any sexual activity outside of a committed relationship, this guy persisted in trying to initiate intimate encounters with me.

When I confronted him about his behaviour and asked for an explanation, he pointed back to his initial statement about not wanting a relationship despite treating me like a girlfriend. He made it clear that he had been honest with me, implying that it was my fault for interpreting things differently.

Wow, what a total player! I blocked and deleted him quickly, but I won't lie; he got into my head.

You need to stick to your boundaries, girl! Trust your gut instincts – if something doesn't feel right, it's probably because it isn't. And here's a wise saying to keep in mind: "When you see life through rose-tinted glasses, those red flags just blend in like any old flag!" So, stay aware and don't let those red flags go unnoticed.

Now that you know what to watch out for, it's time to show any guys with sketchy boundaries who's boss! Show him your unmatched self-assuredness and make it clear that you won't tolerate being messed with. Make sure he understands your clear boundaries, and confidently cut ties with anyone who dares to cross them. You deserve nothing less than respect and healthy, mutually respectful relationships!

Remember, my darling, that you teach people how to treat you, so it's important to never forget that!

CHAPTER

22

"Physical and intellectual attraction"

$\mathcal{I}$'ve been observing people close to me – clients, friends, and family – and I've noticed something interesting. They often make the same mistakes in their relationships. Simply put, after talking to both women and men and watching how things unfold, here's the deal: if you want to keep a guy interested, you must establish a strong level of attraction, regardless of the situation. It's important to remember that attraction can be physical and intellectual.

When a guy's initial physical attraction to a woman begins to fade, it can strain their relationship and increase the likelihood of it ending. However, do you know what changes the game in relationships? Intellectual attraction! That unique quality can take your connection with someone from simply liking them to being completely invested. Of course, physical attraction is important, too, but when you introduce some intellectual sparks into the equation, it takes things to a whole new level!

While looks may be the first thing we notice in a person, forming a genuine connection goes beyond mere appearances. Sharing a deep intellectual bond with someone can elevate your emotions to a whole new level. To create a meaningful relationship, developing an attraction beyond the surface level is important. This deeper connection will ensure that partners feel more involved and committed to each other.

Now that we've covered that, let's take it up a notch and discuss the importance of attraction.

If you want to bring out the best in a man, it's important to show your appreciation without undermining his confidence. Allowing him to be true to himself and embracing his masculinity is a wonderful way to express that appreciation. So, just be yourself and let him do the same!

"Why do certain people feel drawn to each other?"

The common belief is that it all boils down to looks alone, but let me debunk that myth right now. Let's be honest: outward appearances do play a role. I won't sugar-coat it and pretend that men don't care about looks; of course, they do, and it's important to put in at least some effort there, BUT one of my goals is to help you comprehend how men think, including their perspectives on physical attraction because we women tend to over obsess about how we look. We often feel like we do not look good enough and that now man will fancy us.

It's not uncommon for men to have an ideal image of the perfect woman. If you were to ask any guy about his ideal woman's appearance, he would likely list a set of attractive traits. Some may prefer redheads, while others may insist on certain physical features like blue eyes or a larger bust size.

Perhaps he's one of those guys who claims to prefer big bums. But let's not get influenced by what the media feeds us. Those so-called perfect traits are often shaped by magazines, TV, and movies (and perhaps a Kardashian or two).

When it comes to what truly touches his heart, these traits don't matter. Sure, he might have a fleeting fantasy about being with them, but let's be realistic – that's not what will maintain his long-term interest. You just have to think about what your ideal man would look like, then think back on what your previous crushes/ex-partners have looked like ... see what I mean?

You don't have to look like a supermodel to get the attention of amazing guys. If it were only about stunning beauty, there wouldn't be any single actresses or models out there. Women who are cute or charming still have a shot at finding love. Have you ever noticed how many times we read in the papers about a gorgeous model or Movie Star being cheated on or breaking up with their partner? Surprisingly, so many stunning women on TV struggle to find and keep love.

You know what's interesting? We often see these super beautiful movie stars struggling in their love lives, while the more relatable "girl next door" types effortlessly attract admirers.

Beauty isn't all about appearances. It's about how we act and behave, which can make us irresistibly attractive to others. When we're confident and kind and carry ourselves well, we create a magnetic charm that draws people in. Your ability to have engaging conversations, present yourself with style, exude confidence and playfulness, and create a subtle hint of sexual tension contribute to how others see your beauty.

Alright, here's the deal your outer appearance has nothing to do with any of these qualities. While we can't change society's beauty standards, we do have control over how we perceive ourselves. The good news is that our self-perception of beauty matters most when it comes to attraction and relationships. So, focus on embracing your inner beauty and feeling fabulous in your skin!

Attraction is a funny thing, you know. It doesn't always follow the usual rules and can take us by surprise. Sometimes, we are drawn to someone who doesn't fit our typical preferences. It's happened to me as well, like when I'm hanging out with my friends at a bar and we strike up a conversation with some guys. I'll be real with you: There have been times when I've been instantly smitten by someone just because of their good looks.

But let me tell you, looks can be deceiving. It has happened way too often that after talking to someone for just a few minutes, I've realised they are about as interesting as watching paint dry. And yet, their friend next to them, who may not win any beauty contests, has a great sense of humour, a kind heart, and a mischievous twinkle in his eye. Suddenly, my focus shifts towards him, and BOOM! It's like a bolt of lightning striking, and everything changes in a split second!

Before embarking on a mission to captivate others, you must learn to captivate and love yourself first.

I need to stress this again, as it is so important: Make yourself a priority and address any issues or insecurities you may have. Instead of solely fixating on external factors that attract people, dedicate some time to improving the internal aspects of your life. If you're seeking a strong and enduring relationship with a man, getting to know yourself better and wholeheartedly embracing your feelings and emotions is crucial. This self-awareness is the foundation for everything else to naturally fall into place.

Does that make sense?

Good. Let's talk some more…

CHAPTER

23

"Falling in love",

$\mathcal{H}$ ere's a little nugget of wisdom for you. During the first six months of your new relationship, try to hold off on making any major life choices – like moving in together, tying the knot, or even starting a family. Those early days are often filled with intense emotions that can sometimes fog up your judgment. Giving yourself time to understand each other before jumping into serious commitments.

Going back to what I previously said about people jumping from one relationship to another without taking room to breathe in between? From another angle, it's sometimes because they're hooked on the intense high of natural chemicals that surge through their bodies during those initial, thrilling stages of dating. The rush and feelings that race through you are comparable to being on drugs.

On the flip side, have you ever noticed that after being with someone for a few months, even the little things they do that we used to find so cute can start to irritate us? It's like our bodies crave more of the dopamine we had in abundance in the beginning! Romantic books and movies often portray love as the honeymoon phase that lasts forever, but let's be honest, that's complete nonsense. Real love is when the initial excitement fades, and you can still say with a smile, "He is my best friend."

I find it fascinating how our emotions and reactions often follow specific patterns. Love triggers intriguing psychological, chemical, and behavioural changes within us. Our emotions and reactions towards love are intertwined, creating a complex situation. When it comes to being in love, a pretty cool process happens in your brain and body. It involves the release of love chemicals that directly influence your behaviour.

"So, what happens when we fall in love?"

Well, during different relationship stages, our bodies undergo chemical changes. In the beginning, during the wonderful honeymoon stage, when you're head over heels for someone and feel incredibly happy, there are higher levels of three specific chemicals flowing through your veins.

- **Norepinephrine**
- **Dopamine**
- **Serotonin**

I may not be a scientific expert regarding the body's chemical reactions, but who needs all that knowledge when we can simply feel love, right? You can always google that if you're curious about the nitty-gritty details of hormones and chemicals. Instead, let me share the heartfelt responses I received when I asked my loved ones what it feels like to be in love. Their words were truly touching!

"To me, the emotional aspect of love is absolutely incredible. It brings such a comforting sense of security and a warm feeling of 'home.' It's like having my own personal cheerleader who will always be by my side, ready to lend a caring ear and offer companionship whenever I need it. When we chose each other, something magical happened! So, I would say that it's all about feeling safe and supported and knowing that you can choose this person every day for the rest of your life, even when the going gets tough."

~Sarah~

"I fell in love gradually. When you fall in love, it enables you to be vulnerable with someone without the fear of judgment. You can truly be yourself and have open

conversations about anything and everything, knowing that you won't be criticised or judged. Your anxiety and worries diminish because you trust this person and know that they will always be there to support you."

~Belle~

"He puts up with my nonsense. He's patient and kind and would fiercely defend me against anyone he believes has wronged me. He's a bloody nightmare, but damn it, he's MY nightmare, and I'm never letting him go!"

~Danni~

"I adore his little quirks and often find myself smiling at the things he has said or done. Suddenly, many love songs remind me of him. I see him in everything around me. When he is sad or anxious, it pains me as well, and it motivates me to do everything I can to make him feel better."

~Gina~

"We can be completely naked and cuddly, but you know what? That's still not close enough for me. I have this intense feeling that I want to melt into him or become a part of him, making his skin my forever home. It's just so amazing!"

~Naimh~

"I used to be quite cynical when it came to relationships, merely tolerating the men I was with until I inevitably became bored and moved on. But Wowza, this incredible man, has completely changed my perspective! He not only motivates me to strive for greatness, but I can honestly say that I have experienced significant personal growth because of him. He is my true love, and without him, I would feel utterly lost."

~Lilly~

"It's truly humbling. Communication is the cornerstone of our relationship, and when love is right, it brings an incredible sense of peace and calmness. It took me by surprise, as I never could have imagined just how amazing it would be! The love and affection we have for each other is instantly magical. Our paths crossed in the most unexpected manner, with neither of us actively seeking a relationship. But now, our connection is absolutely breathtaking!"

~Nalia~

Love encompasses more than just butterflies in your stomach and sexual chemistry. It delves much deeper than mere physical attraction. It's that moment when you lock eyes with someone, and they truly comprehend you, understanding your every need and desire. Love is about putting each other's happiness above your own. A beautiful blend of respect, trust, and affection creates an extraordinary bond. Love brings warmth and a profound sense of security, even though it can also leave you feeling vulnerable.

PART TWO

Understanding how the male mind works and living in harmony.

CHAPTER
24

"Passive Aggressive No More"

*H*ave you ever wondered why you and your partners have such different perspectives? Well, my darling, I'm here to unravel this mystery for you!

Not everything is black and white; there are many shades of grey. However, when it comes to men and women, they seem to have very little in common apart from belonging to the same species. This is not a sweeping generalisation. Studies have shown significant differences in how a woman's brain functions compared to men's. I believe that men have different wants and needs. Let me explain...

Many years ago, when I worked at a large transport company, I was chatting with a colleague complaining about his wife giving him a hard time for being messy. And you know what? It suddenly dawned on me – sometimes guys aren't avoiding household chores because they're lazy. Nope, brace yourself for this because they simply don't care about them! They don't find any satisfaction with the result and would rather not do any chores because they simply do not care about the mess!

Have you ever been in a relationship where you found yourself, for example, constantly doing all the cooking? It can be frustrating, especially when you put so much effort into planning healthy and delicious meals. But have you ever considered that maybe your partner doesn't even want those dinners? You might unintentionally be getting in the way of his enjoyment of a simple cheese on toast.

Similarly, when you find yourself folding his laundry (another example) to avoid tripping over it, he might think, "Why are you moving my stuff?" It could frustrate him that you've now made it necessary for him to open a drawer to get his top, whereas you are gobsmacked that he is so messy.

Have you also considered that he might WANT the dishes to be put in the sink and left there to soak, just as much as you want them to be washed, dried, and put away in the cupboards? Men often prioritise the present moment, while women tend to plan for the future. We tend to forward think more than guys do, and all we see is that leaving pots in the sink will eventually lead to unpleasant smells and make them harder to clean, but men tend to focus on the present and may not be as concerned about washing up or the potential smell.

Instead of getting all worked up about men not helping with household chores like cleaning and laundry, perhaps we should consider that these tasks may not hold the same importance to them as they do to us. So, rather than expecting him to adhere to OUR standards, it might be easier to find a guy who shares our way of life from the beginning or come to terms with the fact that he may not feel as strongly about these things as you do.

You can spend your life arguing over it or accept him for how he is right now. You may enjoy keeping things clean, so you take care of the cleaning, while he may have strengths, for example, fixing the car, putting up shelves, and carrying the shopping. Just imagine if he was constantly nagging you to build the new chest of drawers from IKEA, even though you didn't even want them in the first place and didn't want to put them together.

I need to clarify: YOU might even be the one who fixes the car, and he likes the clean house while you don't care to be tidy. I am not being old-fashioned; I was just hammering home the point that we cannot expect him to just want what WE want, so if it's important to you, then having opposite values can be a huge deal breaker and make you miserable!

Constantly picking up his dirty pants off the floor, or him going on and on at you constantly moaning about how naturally messy you are, will cause big problems later down the road when then the honeymoon phase is over, and life kicks in.

You must have noticed how guys often ask where something is without looking for it themselves. It can be frustrating. You give them a clear answer like, "It's in the cupboard above the sink". They just open the cupboard and say, "Where?" It's like they expect it to jump out at them or for you to provide a step-by-step guide. Should I whip out a map and draw it for them? It can be quite exasperating, to say the least.

So, the point of what I am saying is that men and women have completely different priorities.

Now, the BIG question is: How do we deal with this so that we can live harmoniously? Earlier, I mentioned that we see things differently and sometimes get moody if a guy doesn't do things the way WE want. However, we can't just ignore our own wants and needs. So, how do we ensure that everyone's needs are met?

Talk about it! Instead of making passive-aggressive comments like, "Oh, I guess I am cooking AGAIN, yeah?" why not try saying something like, "Honey, I have enjoyed cooking for us lately, but would you mind cooking your legendary Spaghetti Bolognese tonight?" And instead of saying, "Oh, will the bins take themselves out?" you could say, "You wouldn't be an angel and take out the bins, would you, darling?"

Men generally appreciate straightforwardness and direct instruction. They may not always pick up on hints, and they dislike passive-aggressive or critical comments and behaviour. Unfortunately, this can sometimes lead to arguments. The solution is to directly ask for what you want and show him how much it/he is appreciated when he delivers! There's no need for any indirect or sarcastic remarks.

CHAPTER 25

"Put yourself in HIS shoes".

So, now we have discovered that men and women have different ways of dealing with emotions and feelings. It's important to remember that this isn't about who is right or wrong. The key is to focus on what produces actual results.

It is easy to say, "Well, it's a two-way street, and guys also need to understand us!" but it is YOU reading this book, so although I agree with that sentiment, we must accept that we cannot change or control other people, we can only control our reaction to them. On that note…

Isn't it true that a woman's love is something quite special? If he's lucky enough to be our guy, we'll move mountains to make him happy. We've got his back through thick and thin. We're right there with him when the going gets tough, cheering him on from the sidelines. When he's under the weather, our hugs are the best medicine, and we're always ready to share a good laugh in happier times and talk over any worries or issues.

If he's feeling low, we know just how to lift his mood. And guess what? Even if he messes up (because let's face it – who doesn't?), we'll still have his back because that's what being in a partnership is all about!

And this is exactly how we expect men to love us in return!! BIG MISTAKE!

Dreaming of a fairy tale love story with your man might not be the most practical expectation. Men and women often express their feelings differently. Men can be more direct, and sometimes they guard their emotions more closely. It can feel like an uphill battle to find a guy who wears his heart on his sleeve.

Even if he's head over heels for you, he might not text you every thirty minutes just to remind you of his love. And it's unlikely that if you have a cold, he'll sit by your side, gently stroking your hair while you recover with a cup of tea and cold compresses. But remember, this doesn't mean he cares any less.

Here's something that truly works:

Before expecting to be understood, try to understand.

Trust me, when you put this into action, it's a game-changer. It has had a greater impact on my relationships with guys than any other piece of advice I've EVER received.

Seriously, you've got to pay attention to this next part...

To truly understand where he's coming from, it's crucial to think outside the box. Don't solely rely on your own opinions or instincts, as that will limit your understanding. It's important to consider his perspective because if you only focus on your own point of view, you might miss out on valuable insights and end up with:

- *Biased opinions.*
- *Judgments.*
- *Disappointment.*

It's completely normal for your thoughts to be limited. After all, they are shaped by your personal experiences and beliefs, aren't they?

"What do you mean, though? How do I change this way of thinking?"

Here's a little example for you: When I'm coaching someone with a different perspective or an issue that I find hard to understand, it's crucial for me to think outside the box and empathise with their point of view. I need to set aside my own opinions, judgments, and expectations regarding the matter so that I can help them.

When my clients speak, I pay careful attention and put my own thoughts and emotions on hold. I really try to see things from their perspective by diving into their thoughts, opinions, history, and expectations (based on what they have told me and the questions I ask them).

Then, I take a moment and put myself in their shoes. Seeing things from their perspective is truly eye-opening. It not only helps me understand them better but can also change my own opinion at times. Furthermore, this approach is incredibly helpful in finding solutions to any issues that may arise. One day, I had a light bulb moment and realised that if you apply the same principle to your partner, you can achieve outstanding results!

I know this may sound deep, but I really want to share more with you. This is where you'll truly learn how to effectively interact with guys and achieve the positive results you crave.

If you want to understand a guy's perspective, start with a genuine and honest conversation. Make sure there are no interruptions, and simply listen to what he has to say. Delve into his likes, dislikes, and expectations to truly comprehend what drives him. Once you have a solid understanding of his mindset, step out of your own shoes and empathise with his point of view.

I understand that sometimes we may not see eye to eye, but it is crucial for us to respect and acknowledge each other's feelings. By taking the time to understand both perspectives, we can find the best way to understand each other.

Trust me, mastering this skill will benefit not only your relationships but also your life overall! I'm not suggesting that you should ignore or forget your own feelings – they are extremely important. However, it can be beneficial for you to consider both sides of the coin. Learning to do this can truly be a life-changing experience.

Here is an example of what happened to me a few years ago ...

Have you ever found yourself trapped in a relationship rut? I can relate, as I experienced it a few years ago myself. Looking back, it is obvious that we were so caught up in our own emotions and thoughts that we neglected to consider each other's perspectives, causing recurring arguments where we were both more concerned with being right and having our say than listening and considering the other's side. But you know what? Making a small shift in my thinking had a huge impact and completely changed the dynamic of our relationship. I will tell you why!

So, it all started when we made a spur-of-the-moment decision to take a weekend trip to Brighton. We were filled with excitement and ready for an adventure. However, as we hit the road, things started to get a bit heated, just like it had been happening a lot recently. Silly arguments broke out over things like directions and where to grab some food.

I won't fib; there were moments of frustration and feeling misunderstood. So, I decided to take a leaf out of my own book – the one I use with my clients. Instead of being absorbed in what I wanted and needed, my feelings and my thoughts, I made a deliberate attempt to see things through his eyes. It wasn't a walk in the park initially, I won't lie, but as the weekend rolled on, it became more and more evident how this shift in viewpoint was making a world of difference.

I made a conscious effort to hear him out without cutting in or making assumptions, seeing it from my own point of view or putting words in his mouth (I'll be honest, it was tough, but I pulled it off). This method truly helped me grasp his emotions and the things that were bothering him. It came as a surprise that he'd been feeling swamped with his workload and had some staff issues recently, and all he had been hoping for was some stress-free quality time together.

As the weekend unfolded, I found myself considering his preferences alongside my own when making plans. We went on a hike at his favourite location before he insisted on dining at the upscale restaurant that was my first choice. Surprisingly, we also dabbled in some activities he'd been keen to try but hadn't because I wasn't initially interested. To my delight, it was a blast! Plus, who knew I had such a knack for table tennis?

Isn't it amazing how quickly things can change? As soon as I began to take his feelings and needs into account, just as much as my own, our connection deepened. And guess what happened next? He started putting MY feelings first! We shared laughter that seemed endless, our communication reached new heights, and it felt like with each passing moment, our love was growing even deeper.

As our journey wrapped up, we didn't just resolve our early disagreements but also found fresh respect for each other's viewpoints. It was a timely nudge, reminding us that relationships are built on the pillars of compromise, understanding and empathy.

Taking a moment to step back and see things from your partner's perspective can work wonders for your relationship. When we make an effort to understand where our partner is coming from, it opens up a whole new world of empathy and connection.

You might be surprised at how this simple change in viewpoint can bring about a positive transformation in your relationship. Now, I want to make something clear: appreciating your partner's perspective doesn't mean neglecting your own needs. It's all about finding that perfect balance. So, take the time to understand each other's viewpoints, communicate your own needs, and work together towards a relationship that satisfies both of you. Trust me, it's worth it.

CHAPTER
26

"Are you the cool chick?"

*E*ver heard a guy refer to a girl as a 'cool chick'? You know, something like, "Oh, Lisa? Yeah, she's cool!" It might sound like just an offhand comment, but when a man uses this phrase about a woman, it reveals something quite intriguing. It suggests that he finds her truly captivating and is genuinely drawn to her.

When guys say "cool," what they mean is that the woman understands them and is fun and easy to get on with. She has an incredible ability to grasp the complexities of men's social and emotional realms. It's as if she effortlessly navigates challenging situations and handles them like a total pro. When they use that word, they're essentially giving her a virtual high-five for being so amazing!

If you hear a guy referring to a woman as "cool," trust me, he low-key wants to be with her.

She's super easy to connect with, and every time he has a chat with her, time just flies by. And if there is a disagreement or some issue she wants to raise, she can do it in a way which does not come across as confrontational or overly critical. She is able to stand her ground on the things that matter to her, and yet not in a way that has him instantly put his guard up, feeling like he is being attacked. The holy grail! Maybe it's because they have loads of shared interests and can't stop talking, or maybe it's simply because she's so captivating and relatable that he could happily listen to her for hours on end.

She's got a fantastic sense of humour! He can tease and roast her, he doesn't feel like he is on eggshells, he can relax and be himself, and she'll take it all in good fun. The best part is she's got an edgy and darker sense of humour herself. Unlike those who get easily offended or anxiously overthink things, she doesn't let things get to her. Let's be honest here: guys can sometimes be a bit clueless and insensitive when it comes to women. But hey, they do appreciate it when someone sets them straight when they go too far. Luckily, this cool girl knows her boundaries and can dish out jokes just as well as anyone else!

She's hilarious, just like I said earlier. It's incredible when a girl has a talent for making a guy laugh till his stomach hurts. Not that I'm saying women aren't funny, but we usually play it safe with jokes. But you know what? A cool girl always goes for it, whether she nails the punchline or not!

She's super open-minded and always up for trying new things, whether it's jumping out of a plane, eating fiery hot food, or even getting a bit adventurous in the bedroom. She doesn't back down from exciting experiences and enjoys taking charge. Guys absolutely adore it when a girl pushes them out of their comfort zone because, let's be real, they could easily stay in their cosy bubble forever without a gentle push.

This woman is never shy about expressing her thoughts and has an infectious sense of humour. She's got this knack for knowing just how much she can bend the rules and when it's the right time to do so. When she's in a playful mood, she fearlessly steps over lines like a child engrossed in a game of hopscotch. It keeps things lively because you're always guessing what she'll say next – it certainly keeps everyone on their toes! And let me assure you, if anyone dares to cross her, they should brace themselves for her outspoken response (and be ready for everyone else to hear about it, too)!

And finally, the golden rule: She's totally down-to-earth and super chill.

So, what do we learn from this cool girl? Well, most men simply want a woman who supports them without trying to take control of everything, without seemingly criticising them constantly, without making the smallest things into the biggest arguments. Somebody they can relax with and be themselves with. They desire a strong and independent partner who can take care of themselves in this crazy world.

However, they also appreciate a woman who knows how to make them feel like they're the most important person in her life. It's not about being afraid to show vulnerability or being gentle with him. When a man is with this amazing girl, it's all about positive vibes, having a great time, and simply enjoying each other's company. Her refreshing energy is something any guy can't help but adore.

So, the uptake is: If you put in the effort to get inside a guy's head and understand what makes him tick, you can create stronger connections with him. And that means building relationships that are based on the real, genuine you – those unique qualities that make you who you are.

Yeah, that's right…

Have you ever been in a situation where you're having a passionate discussion, and the person you're talking to suddenly shuts down or becomes annoyed for no apparent reason? It can be incredibly frustrating, but there's often a deeper reason behind their reaction. It's possible that something you said triggered a past experience for them, which is now influencing how they're responding. Believe me, I've been there too!

On that note, when a guy says something that instantly reminds you of a negative aspect of your past, and it sends shivers down your spine, then remember, while it may cause this initial reaction in you, it is important to realise he is not your ex-boyfriend, he is not your father. The past formed who you are today, but it doesn't need to control who you are tomorrow. This is not to dismiss or disregard such triggers and past experiences but to try to remind yourself that the guy in front of you is not responsible for them. It wasn't him. It isn't him. It's not him!

If you're scratching your head, trying to understand what goes on in a man's mind, don't bother analysing little things! Men have always had their own unique way of thinking, and that's just how they are wired. It's one of those things we must accept! Once you start embracing this fact, you'll be well on your way to figuring out how to attract and maintain commitment in a relationship.

Ever noticed how men seem to live in their own unique world? It's usually filled with sports, banter about football, boasting about their latest car or boat, the Roman Empire, and a healthy dose of competition. Now, imagine if we ladies had to immerse ourselves in that world every day – it could get a bit monotonous, couldn't it? But for the guys? They seem to thrive on it and genuinely enjoy their time in this realm of theirs.

Also, isn't it a bit sad how guys often seem to be experts at concealing their genuine feelings? It's as if society has handed them this unwritten rule that they must keep everything under wraps. This can lead many men to feel somewhat detached and even struggle to comprehend their own emotions. So, it's hardly surprising that when we venture into the world of dating and relationships, both men and women can find it challenging to truly "get" each other.

Let's be honest: finding a decent, good-looking guy who has his life together can sometimes feel like trying to find a needle in a haystack! And let me tell you, finding one who is also ready to settle down soon is even harder! The rarest of all is a man who is on the same page as you when it comes to committing to a relationship or marriage within a similar timeframe.

So, here's the thing: about 90% of guys prefer to remain single or keep things casual until they have a compelling reason to commit. However, let's face it, many of them struggle with determining when it's the right time to settle down. Some may not even know what qualifies as a valid reason.

Have you ever heard of guys chilling together, having a laugh over a game and a cold one, and opening up to each other about their dreams of finding that special someone for the long haul? This occurrence is as infrequent as winning the Lottery... TWICE!!

But you've heard men engaging in conversations about the latest football match, their job, the newest phone they've got their hands on, or a mate's flashy new motor, right? This is often dubbed as "bloke banter". Men and women have different ways of thinking, interacting, and communicating. Men can find it challenging to connect with their emotions, feelings, and deeper meanings, and that's just a fact.

So, if your man struggles to even consider his feelings, how could he possibly answer a question as emotionally complex as his feelings towards you and your relationship?

If you've ever asked your partner about his feelings for you, hoping for a response that truly reflects his love and care, then you'll understand what I'm saying here. The responses from men when asked about their feelings are often far from what a woman wants to hear. Men can sometimes struggle with being open about these things, and there's a reason for this...

CHAPTER
27

"Understand, to be understood".

A lot of men find it challenging to comprehend the depth of our emotions. Rather than seeking to understand us, they sometimes write it off as needless drama. There's a common perception among some men that we women tend to overreact or are excessively dramatic.

It is a blatant fact that men and women often have very different ways of expressing their feelings. When it comes to dealing with problems, men often lean towards logic and finding solutions, while women tend to seek emotional support and empathy by talking or shedding odd tears. I mean, don't get it twisted; guys also need to wise up and realise that they should try to understand what women like. It's a two-way street, you know? But that's a whole 'nother book!

Let's discuss what truly matters when it comes to finding your Mr. Right! Here are some statements for you to consider:

1. If you're hoping to change how a man sees you, the trick is to start by changing how you see HIM. It's all about shifting your perspective first. Once you do that, it can have a ripple effect and influence how they perceive you as well.

2. If you're seeking genuine change in your life, it begins by adjusting your own behaviour. We can't control others, but we have complete control over how we choose to react to them.

3. If you're really looking for change, it's time to shake things up in your own mind. Start questioning your mindset and how you perceive things outside of the box.

4. If you are hoping to have him listen more to you or see things more from your point of view, again, you need to offer the same to him first. And yes, yes, 'not fair, why me first?' But this book is about what YOU can do.

There is a clear theme in that list: the need for change starts from within yourself. Managing to change someone else is about as likely as seeing a flying elephant!

OK, so, we have now covered why men are like they are, and we have looked at the fact that the change you want needs to come from yourself first. We now need to delve into the male dating mind!

The truth is, there are many guys out there who can be called serial daters. They have a fear of being alone, so they quickly move from one 'situationship' to another without taking much time for themselves. If you happen to meet a guy on a dating app, chances are you're one of several he swiped right on and messaged, and one of many he plans to meet if given the opportunity. Men often play the 'numbers' game in online dating, sending the same message to multiple girls in the hopes of getting a response. It's like casting a line into a pond, hoping to catch something!

Even if you happen to meet him in real life, outside of the dating app world, it's safe to assume that there are other women on his phone. Even if a guy is going through a dry spell with no romantic prospects, he'll still be keeping his options open. For example, how many times have you heard or said this? ....

"This guy seemed so into me, constantly messaging and calling. We were even planning a holiday together." Then, out of the blue, it quickly turns into, *"He's gone cold and suddenly ghosting me. What did I do wrong?"*

It can be incredibly disappointing to feel let down after getting your hopes up, especially when you value honesty and attention. It's disheartening to discover that it feels like 8 out of 10 men are not genuine in their intentions.

Sometimes, as women, we tend to believe that a guy is completely enamoured with us. However, little do we know that he might be comparing us to another woman who ends up winning him over by knowing how to charm him better. It's a tough reality to accept, but it happens more often than we'd like to admit.

Some men believe it's wiser to take their time and carefully evaluate all their choices before committing to one specific girl. You see, girls tend to receive plenty of attention from interested men, so they can choose the ones they really like early on.

On the other hand, some guys receive less attention, so when they do find a girl who's interested, they tend to jump on it and decide later if they're genuinely interested. This is why many girls end up getting ghosted!

"So, how can I stand out and ensure that he only dates me?"

The key is to understand how he perceives you. When you first meet a guy, you both start from the same place, just like any other woman he might come across.

If a guy starts showing interest in you before you have even really had a conversation, it's likely because he's initially attracted to what you look like as that is the first thing we see when we meet someone (stands to reason)

However, to go beyond that initial attraction, it's important to show him more than just your physical appearance. Focus on building a connection with him through meaningful conversations and shared interests. Let him see your unique personality, sense of humour, and intelligence. Be confident and genuine, allowing him to witness the amazing qualities that set you apart from others. Remember, it's not solely about being physically attractive to him. It's about forging a deeper connection and showcasing the qualities that make you truly special.

Men come in all sorts of shapes and sizes, just like women do. And you know what? Each man has his own unique preferences when it comes to the type of woman he finds attractive. It's all about personal taste! You will hear one guy raving about a girl's big booty. Well, another guy will be turned off by a big butt.

So, here's the truth: ANY woman who has the confidence to put herself out there and highlight her best qualities can easily find some dates. It's all about being confident and embracing what makes you unique. You do NOT need to be a supermodel to find love, ladies. That's a fact! In fact, one of the most important things about plucking and preening, dressing up and working out, is not actually about how we look to the guy at all. It is about how we feel about ourselves. Our own self confidence. I mean, how many times have you heard a guy say, 'Wow she had lovely eyebrows?'

Now that we've cleared that up, let's shift our focus to what I've learned and studied about the male thought process when he's dating you. Don't worry if you're part of the 99. 8% who haven't quite figured out the intricacies of attraction and meeting men. It's never too late to get a crash course, and rest assured, you're in good hands.

Spoiler alert: it's the opposite of what you think!!

CHAPTER

28

"The emotional gap"

*B*ased on my extensive experience of spending over 30 years at the 'dating school of hard knocks' (and graduating with honours), I can confidently tell you that our desires, drives, preferences, strengths, weaknesses, behaviours, and personality traits are primarily influenced by a combination of our DNA and how we were raised in society. It's a blend of nature and nurture that ultimately shapes who we are.

Ever wondered why men and women seem to express themselves differently? It's quite fascinating, isn't it? We women often have our own unique way of communicating, with a secret language that men sometimes struggle to understand. We can delve into the tiniest details that guys may find unimportant. On the other hand, men tend to be more concise and less interested in discussing personal matters. It's a bit strange, isn't it?

Well, let me share my perspective on this whole thing:

Guys have been stuck in the same old role for, like, forever. It's been going on for thousands of years and doesn't seem to be changing anytime soon. Even though technology has drastically transformed the way we live, our fundamental human traits remain unchanged. Our brains have various components that generate motivations and cravings for different things. Interestingly, these desires often clash with each other.

Think about it: a guy may want a bad-ass, self-sufficient lady to be his partner. But at the same time, he might also crave that sense of being indispensable and relied upon by her. He might enjoy the attention, yet secretly desire to be seen as someone who doesn't necessarily require it. Yeah, women face their fair share of conflicts too, just in different areas than men.

Conflicts can indeed arise between men and women, but the areas where they tend to occur may differ. I often hear women expressing frustration about the confusing situations that men create when it comes to relationships and interactions. Navigating through these situations can be a real struggle.

"Why do men find it challenging to choose between a strong, self-assured woman and a relaxed, easy-going one?"

Well, here's the thing: both situations fulfil important social and emotional needs for men, even if it may sound a bit strange and contradictory. Independent women give men a sense of freedom and the feeling of not being tied down. However, when women ask for or value his help and support, it can truly make him feel strong and masculine.

For that reason, it is understandable why some individuals might find women who possess a combination of independence and occasional dependency quite intriguing. However, it can be a bit confusing for us to comprehend, as not all of us share the same desires and needs, you know?

At times, establishing effective communication and emotional connections with men can be challenging. Bridging the gap between our differences can feel like a daunting task. However, there is no need to worry! Undoing it is simpler than you may think. By making a few simple changes in your approach, you can pave the way for happier relationships.

I'll explain it ...

Have you ever met someone who appears to have it all, but deep down, they're still not happy or satisfied? We all know at least one person like that, don't we? You've likely, over the years, encountered other women who aren't satisfied with their relationship. They always seem to crave more and never seem content with what they have. Maybe you've even felt this way yourself?

"So, what's the deal here and what can we do about it?"

The reason behind this is quite simple for many women: they struggle to find true happiness in their relationships or even on a personal level because they constantly compare the present reality with an idealised image, they have in their mind of how things should be. It seems that they are constantly measuring their partner against an unrealistic standard.

When women compare their ideal expectations to the reality they face, it can be incredibly discouraging and frustrating. It appears there is an emotional gap between the vision women have for themselves and the experiences men encounter. This gap can deplete their energy and leave them feeling frustrated.

But guess what…

Ideals and reality often don't align. It's no secret that what we envision doesn't always match what happens. When a guy's ideals are completely different from yours, it can be tricky to navigate. However, the key is to understand and respect each other's differences. It's important to have open and honest conversations, listen to each other's viewpoints, and find common ground. By considering this idea, you can improve the way you interact with guys and how your emotions influence your actions.

I understand that it might sound a bit strange but hear me out. Your dreams and ideals are important, especially when it comes to relationships. Like I have said earlier, it's completely normal and totally fine for you to visualise your ideal situation with a man. It can be a healthy way to stay motivated and inspired as you shape your future goals. But here's the thing - sometimes it can be difficult to feel happy in your relationship and life when you constantly compare them to your fantasy world and always feel like it is lacking.

It's kind of like feeling let down when your partner doesn't bring you flowers every week, or he doesn't notice your new hairdo. But honestly, those things aren't everything. What truly matters is whether he's there for you when life throws you a curveball or takes care of you when you're feeling unwell. It's about seeing things as they are and not getting too caught up in idealisations. I completely understand where you're coming from. It's natural to have certain expectations and desires in a relationship, like the small gestures or the little things that make us feel special. However, it's important to remember that true connection goes beyond these surface-level gestures.

I can tell you first-hand that the key to a successful relationship is having a supportive partner who stands by you through life's ups and downs (and believe me, there will be many). It is important to find a man who understands your needs, supports you, and remains by your side during difficult times, like a two-man army.

So, instead of getting caught up in idealised versions of what a partner should be based on movies or romantic books, it's about finding someone who truly sees and accepts you, flaws and all. Ultimately, the deeper emotional connection is what truly matters. Knowing that your partner will be there for you through thick and thin and that you can completely rely on them is invaluable. This kind of bond is priceless. So, while it's natural to desire small acts of love and attention, it's important to be aware that these superficial needs are ego-based and not the real deal.

It's worth pointing out that men also do the same thing.

You know those guys who are always searching for something better, even when they're already with an amazing partner? It's like they believe they'll magically stumble upon a beautiful Instagram model who will love them unconditionally without expecting anything in return. Pretty crazy, right? Men often have this fantasy of finding the perfect woman, but let's face it, she doesn't exist either. It's super important not to get caught up in chasing an unrealistic dream, and it's a surefire way to NOT find happiness.

Don't be the female version of that guy who's always chasing after an imaginary ideal. Instead, focus on internalising a few important ideas that will help you connect with attractive emotions and emotional states. If you want to have an irresistible charm and attract guys for all the right reasons, here are some tips to help you stand out from the crowd of other women:

- Embrace your authenticity! Be true to yourself and let your unique personality shine.
- Cultivating confidence is key: Believe in yourself and proudly showcase your self-assurance.
- Develop a positive mindset.
- Show genuine interest.
- Engage in meaningful conversations and show genuine interest in him.
- Take care of yourself by prioritising self-care and presenting your best self.

By following these tips, you will definitely make a lasting impression and attract the attention of the right kind of guy.

CHAPTER 29

"The guys come flocking".

$\mathcal{A}$s I have already mentioned, on the first meeting men are initially attracted to a woman's appearance (although it's important to remember that different guys have different preferences). However, this initial attraction tends to fade as time goes on. What truly creates lasting infatuation is the essence of who you are as a person.

Guys are naturally attracted to confident, genuinely funny, and intelligent women who don't rely on them or anyone else. They want a girl who can be their best friend while also creating a lot of sexual tension. Someone who brings unique and adventurous experiences into their lives and challenges them to break free from old stereotypes. She doesn't have to act like a bimbo or play games, and she couldn't care less about seeking social validation as long as she's happy. Those are the kind of women that guys fall head over heels for. Boom!

Here's a little nugget of wisdom for you: don't let anyone else define how you should behave. Embrace your true self, just as you are right now, not the version of yourself that could exist if you altered your appearance or shed a few pounds! Confidence is everything, so celebrate who you are and ignore those glossy magazines trying to pigeonhole you. Live life by your own rules. And remember this: You might be the juiciest apple in the orchard, but not everyone is fond of apples!!

Let us discuss how to attract men and build amazing long-term relationships. There are two important factors to consider.

Firstly, your emotional state plays a significant role. It encompasses your attitude, communication style, self-perception, confidence level, and even your personality. These intangible qualities make you exceptional. So, remember, when it comes to achieving success in relationships, it goes beyond mere looks or superficial aspects. How you feel about yourself truly matters more than you may even realise!

Secondly, your behaviour and communication style with guys can be a deal breaker. This is influenced by your self-awareness and personal growth. However, there are other important aspects to consider, a lot of which we have already covered here, such as understanding what attracts men. Ultimately, it's a process of becoming more self-aware and adjusting your inner thoughts, feelings, beliefs, and self-perception. It's all about delving deep into that "self-awareness" stuff. But before you can truly master how you interact and communicate with men, certain things need to happen first.

You know how emotions can completely take over and spread like wildfire, don't you? They have this incredible ability to influence the people around you. Let's talk about being excited for a moment - when you're super hyped up, those nearby can't help but catch that same energy and get pumped, too! However, when you're feeling down, guys can sense it and react accordingly. Some might match your mood and be there for you, while others might withdraw a bit. If you want to create a positive vibe with a guy, simply setting a positive emotional tone is an easy-peasy way to go about it.

I'm sure you're familiar with how these things work and come across them all the time, so I won't bore you with the basics. But I have a feeling that you're looking for more than just putting on a happy face and getting a guy's attention, am I right? Good.

One of my friends, Sam, once shared with me the story of how he met the love of his life:

So, picture this: I'm walking home from work, minding my own business, when I witness a rather amusing scene. This girl in front of me snaps the heel on her shoe and takes a tumble headfirst; she goes down with a bang. Now, normally, I would rush over to check if she's okay, but before I can even react, she looks up at me with the biggest grin on her face. And let me tell you, she's not your typical "conventional" beauty - she's a bit on the heavier side and not the most graceful with her stumble. But here's the thing: instead of feeling embarrassed or trying to hide it, she's all smiles and couldn't care less about what anyone thinks of her. And you know what? That kind of confidence instantly made her attractive in my eyes.

They got married two years after that meeting and now have twin boys!

It's important to recognise that attraction goes beyond mere physical appearance. It's a powerful emotion that pulls you towards someone, almost like a magnetic force. Individuals who possess attractiveness radiate a certain charm that compels you to be in their company.

Being in the presence of someone fulfils an emotional need within you. However, attraction is not solely dependent on looks. Someone who can brighten your day, regardless of their physical appearance, can have the same effect. On the other hand, even if someone is good-looking, but their personality is unpleasant, it's better to admire them from a distance!

CHAPTER

30

"Feminine or masculine energy?"

It's quite amusing how we women are often drawn to "manly" or "masculine" men but then find ourselves annoyed when these men don't show enough emotions. Ever wonder why guys appear calm amid emotional dramas? It's as if they retreat into their own little world, attempting to compose their feelings and navigate the complexities of relationships. You must have you noticed how guys can get a bit annoyed when us ladies seek deep emotional connections and meaning in life? It can be frustrating for both sides because we struggle to see things from each other's perspective.

Let's take a moment to reflect on this:

There is often an expectation for men to be tough and conceal their emotions. We desire them to embody the image of fearless warriors, giving us a sense of security. However, we also expect them to be sensitive and emotional when we require their support.

The key to attracting masculine men is embracing our feminine energy. We all have a blend of both masculine and feminine energies within us. It's like having two vibes that coexist in each person. Just to clarify, these energies are not linked to gender, but one energy usually takes the lead.

"But what do these energies actually mean? And how do they impact relationships?"

Well, if you're seeking balance and harmony in your love life, it's crucial to grasp the distinction between masculine and feminine energy. Masculine energy is assertive, logical, and action-oriented, while feminine energy is intuitive, nurturing, and receptive.

Understanding these differences can greatly enhance your love life.

We often associate masculinity with males and femininity with females, but it may surprise you to know that your gender doesn't determine the type of energy you possess. Regardless of whether you're male or female, everyone has a combination of both masculine and feminine energies within them. How these energies manifest can vary from person to person, but they are present in all of us. By recognising this distinction, you can gain a better understanding of yourself and learn how to access each energy when necessary.

"What is Masculine Energy?"

Masculine energy is characterised by acting, being proactive, and getting things done. It embodies strength, stability, and reliability, along with qualities like determination, clarity of mind, and laser focus. This energy naturally excels at setting up systems, making rules, and using logic to approach tasks intelligently. Key characteristics of masculine energy include:

- Good rational and logical skills.
- Ability to think clearly.
- Ability to build ongoing effort.
- Good external strength.
- The ability to think creatively and solve problems.
- Fondness of difficult challenges.
- The longing for admiration and appreciation.

- Fierce independence.

"So, what's the deal with feminine energy? What makes it different from everything else?"

Feminine energy is like a breath of fresh air, distinct from masculine energy. It brings a fluid and vibrant essence, adding a unique touch to everything. The way this energy flows cannot always be predicted or explained with logic. A common misconception about feminine energy is that it revolves around waiting for Prince Charming to charge in on his trusty steed and sweep you off your feet. But let me tell you, that's not the case at all!

Feminine energy is all about embracing your inner strength and power while staying open to love and connection. It's about being a strong, empowered woman who knows her desires and takes charge of her life and relationships. Instead of being passive, it's about being proactive and pursuing what you want.

You don't need to be desperate or chase after men; let them take the lead. Being feminine is about being in control, going after your desires, and refusing to settle for anything less.

If you have a dominant feminine energy, you may notice some of these traits in yourself:

- Good at taking care of yourself and showing yourself some love.
- Calming down effortlessly seems to be your thing.
- Able to be empathetic.
- Capable of making decisions that surpass rationality.
- Making your own feelings a top priority.
- Being able to communicate well.

- Able to find creative inspiration.

Now that you're aware, it's interesting to note how men and women have their own distinct styles of communication. It's not surprising that they often have contrasting approaches when you consider the differences in masculine and feminine energy.

Understanding this is your first step to learning how to get better results with dating guys. Being oblivious to this fact is where things can sometimes go south.

Let's explore some ways in which men and women think differently...

Women have an innate ability to perceive and understand the emotions of others. We have an incredible knack for deciphering people's emotions with just a quick glance at their faces. It's almost like having a superpower! We can effortlessly sense what others are feeling by simply looking into their eyes. But have you ever noticed that guys sometimes struggle with understanding what's going on with the females in their lives?

Put it this way: I can be at a party with a female friend, and even if we're on opposite sides of the room, we can communicate just through eye contact. We have silent conversations with knowing glances, subtle nods, wide eyes, and mischievous smiles that say so much without uttering a word. We would burst into laughter at the same thing, even when standing 10 feet apart and not saying a single word!

It's amusing how it appears that we have this uncanny ability to understand a secret language while men are completely clueless about the intricate communication happening right in front of them. They just can't pick up on the subtle hints we ladies exchange, like a raised eyebrow that basically says, "Let's get out of here NOW!" or a little twinkle in our eyes that means, "I've got your back on this, babe" or even widened eyes that scream, "I can't believe you just said that she has big feet!"

So, if we expect guys to understand our subtle emotions when we're angry or upset, we're going to be consistently disappointed. I've learned (the hard way) that we need to clearly explain to men how we're feeling and why we feel that way. As frustrating as it is, they just don't pick up on the cues like our girlfriends do! Let's talk about why that may be...

"Here's a little history lesson to help us understand why men think the way they do."

To help you understand better, let's take a trip back in history and explore why men might express their feelings differently compared to women. Gaining a deeper understanding of this topic will answer many questions and provide clarity from my perspective.

Let's take a moment to reflect on this: From the very beginning, boys are exposed to various opinions on what it means to be a "real man." They are taught to be tough, confront challenges directly, persevere, and not allow others to take advantage of them. Shed a tear? Absolutely not! They are raised to believe in rolling up their sleeves and getting things done. Whether it's doing household maintenance, handling heavy lifting, dealing with snow, or mowing the lawn – they truly appreciate the value of hard work.

When you think about it, you will realise how men must navigate through rules and expectations that women NEVER have to encounter. You know, there's this unwritten rule in life that seems to be exclusively shared with boys. From a young age, he's taught to be the protector of his family, looking out for his mother and younger siblings while ensuring the safety of their home. The whole point of these teachings is to get him ready for one thing: BEING A MAN!

"So, why does this matter?"

Well, my darling, if you can manage to understand, it will really help you live more harmoniously with your dream guy. You've probably noticed the unwritten rule in our society that men are discouraged from freely expressing their emotions. It's as if there's a secret agreement they're expected to adhere to.

From a young age, boys are often taught the notion that being a "real man" means keeping their emotions hidden. You've probably heard it too - mothers advising their sons to toughen up, and fathers encouraging them not to cry with the attitude that "real men don't cry." It seems like society expects them to conceal or disregard their feelings simply because they are male.

Moms have a knack for influencing their sons' emotions, often without even realising it. Dads also play a role in this dynamic. They enjoy rough-and-tumble fun with their boys, but with their daughters, they tend to be gentler and more caring. As children grow up, parents unknowingly discourage boys from showing vulnerability while encouraging girls to express themselves freely.

So, can you see where I'm going with this? Males and females are treated differently from birth, like chalk and cheese. I mean, is it any wonder that we don't "get" each other? How do you get through to him? Let's talk about that...

CHAPTER

31

"Is being attractive a curse?"

*A*lright, now that we've established the crucial role of attraction, let's dive into some specific actions that can effortlessly grab a guy's attention. These actions not only create attraction but can also take it to the next level!

You know what? Failing isn't always such a bad thing. Surprisingly, it can be incredibly helpful in life! It's during those moments of making mistakes that we learn valuable lessons and experience personal growth. I can tell you first-hand that most of my most valuable life lessons have come from mistakes or bad situations.

Here's a fun fact: many remarkable women I know have made their fair share of mistakes in their careers, finances, and relationships. But here's the thing: they all share an important trait - they learn from their mistakes quickly! They won't make the same mistake twice. So, even if these women find themselves in a similar situation, you can be sure that their reactions won't be identical.

"So, what is the secret to getting a guy's attention?"

Well, have you ever noticed how often a guy will leave a drop-dead gorgeous woman and end up marrying someone who may be considered average-looking? I've witnessed it countless times.

Men are naturally drawn to women who possess emotional stability and know how to conduct themselves. They seek a partner who not only makes a great companion but also stimulates them intellectually and supports them fiercely. It can be disheartening to think that not everyone is blessed with good looks or a captivating personality that effortlessly attracts an ideal partner.

Let me ask you a question: Have you ever encountered a woman who effortlessly captivates the attention of men from all directions? It's not just about her face or body - there's something about her personality that works like magic, even if she doesn't conform to conventional beauty standards. She didn't acquire these extraordinary skills from books or advice from others; somehow, she has this innate talent for attracting, engaging in conversation with, and understanding men.

The power to captivate others isn't solely dependent on outward appearance but rather a combination of charisma, confidence, and genuine connection. Some women have mastered the art of being themselves and embracing their unique qualities, which naturally draws men towards them. What makes them stand out? Well, they excel at engaging in meaningful conversations and connecting with guys on a deeper level with confidence. They have a natural understanding of men's emotions, desires, and perspectives, which enables them to forge genuine connections based on empathy and mutual understanding.

It's important to remember that these skills aren't acquired overnight or from external sources alone. They come from within - a blend of self-awareness, self-assurance, and emotional intelligence. By embracing their authentic selves and radiating positivity, they effortlessly attract attention. So, take inspiration from these captivating women! Embrace your OWN uniqueness, continuously strive for personal growth, develop your communication skills, and cultivate empathy towards others' experiences – all while staying true to yourself. Remember that you, too, have the potential to captivate those around you with your own special qualities!

These women aren't some mystical beings with secret powers that instantly make men interested in them. They're just regular people like you and me, doing their own thing.

"So, what is their secret... tell me!"

Well, darling, the truth is, they don't let their fears and personal issues affect how they behave around guys, and they aren't worried about other people's opinions. Their past doesn't hold them back from creating a fun and exciting atmosphere with men. They prefer to keep their initial interactions short and enjoyable. This lady is truly unpredictable, always keeping him on his toes with her next move. She has an uncanny ability to understand what makes men tick without appearing desperate or overly sexual. It's as if she effortlessly attracts them, naturally grasping the dynamics of attraction. If you know a woman like this, then she could be the person who can help you.

"How can knowing this type of woman benefit me?"

Well, here's how: if you know an awesome single lady like that, why not learn from her? Give her a call and propose the idea of a night out. Choose a venue where you usually come across single guys in your age group. Once you're there, just relax, let things happen naturally, and see how it goes. This girl is seriously skilled at sparking interesting conversations with guys - she effortlessly grabs their attention! That's where all the excitement happens, and you can learn a thing or two from her.

Take note of how she carries herself, her body language, and the way she effortlessly interacts with everyone around her - whether it's the bartender or the person next to her. Pay attention to her fearlessness in engaging with men who approach her. These subtle cues offer a glimpse into her natural talent for connecting with guys and capturing their attention when she's interested in someone.

Once you have discovered her expertise, it's time to give it a try yourself! Take inspiration from her natural talent and incorporate it into your own approach. It's all about the energy you're giving off. If you're shy or insecure, you might be guarding yourself and not seem as open, which could give the impression that you're not interested. Work on being more open and maintaining eye contact, and you'll see things change. Embrace your unique qualities and use them to connect with others in an authentic and captivating way. Confidence is the key!

"But what if I just don't feel attractive enough for someone to be interested in me?"

Well, my dear buttercup, you'll already know that physically attractive women often find it easier to attract men…

BUT… and this is a big BUT…

I've noticed something quite fascinating: sometimes, attractive women may face MORE challenges in finding the right partner compared to those who don't receive as much attention. It's an intriguing phenomenon. What I've observed is that women who aren't approached as frequently are often skilled at distinguishing between good and not-so-good men. They also possess the ability to create the ideal conditions for a relationship to flourish.

What's going on here? It feels a bit strange. Lately, I've been thinking about this more, and I've started to notice a recurring pattern. It's quite ironic, but for women who are considered physically attractive, their looks can sometimes prevent them from forming a deeper kind of attraction. It seems that there's more to it than just being good-looking.

"You need to explain more."

Well, let me introduce you to the confident woman. You already know her. You've seen her. She's the one who effortlessly captivates great men and commands attention wherever she goes. You can't help but wonder, "How does she do it? What makes her so special? What secrets does she hold?"

You may have even expressed your frustration to your girlfriends, wondering why men don't seem to notice what an amazing catch YOU are. They may have even reassured you by saying, "He doesn't know what he's missing."

But what if there was a way to make him notice you? Well, here's the thing…

It's no secret that catching a man's eye CAN be as simple as getting him interested in your looks. I mean, it's predictable – men usually respond to what women look like. But here's where things get a bit complicated... If a guy shows interest based on looks alone, it can give you the impression that you're making progress in building a connection with him. Unfortunately, the result is nowhere near what you had hoped for in your love life. While catching his attention through your appearance can be a starting point, it's important to remember that true connections are built on much more than just looks.

Building genuine connections takes time and effort. It involves getting to know someone beyond their physical appearance and understanding their values, interests, and personality. Focus on embracing and showcasing your authentic self and engaging in meaningful conversations that go beyond surface-level interactions.

My sage advice is to prioritise being genuine, kind-hearted, and confident in who you are and how you look. Your true essence will always be more captivating than just your looks. Embrace your inner beauty as it radiates through your actions, words, and the way you treat others. That is how you will meet your soulmate. Quality over quantity every time! Remember, a solid foundation for a strong, lasting relationship (which I am sure is what you want) is built upon substance and shared values rather than superficiality alone.

CHAPTER

32

"Push and Pull"

*F*inding the perfect match isn't always easy, believe me. As a breakup coach with years of experience, I've witnessed it all. But let me share what I've discovered: most guys are searching for that one special lady with whom they can build a strong and meaningful relationship. Yes, even those "player" types have their moments and eventually desire something genuine and committed. However, there's a small twist to this story.

If a guy isn't completely sure about committing to a relationship and all that it entails, he's going to have a tough time fully dedicating himself and making it work. And this isn't just about wanting a relationship either. Even men who genuinely desire a strong and lasting connection can still face challenges in maintaining one.

"So, how do you know if you've found a guy who's ready?"

Well, if he constantly calls you up and asks you out on proper dates and makes an effort, it's pretty clear that he likes you. However, if you find yourself doubting him, feeling anxious, and seeking advice from your friends, then sorry to break it to you, but chances are, he's just not interested!

I know that quite a few women believe that offering a man sex will make him desire her more. **However, the opposite is true (read that again)**. A man truly appreciates what he has to work for. He needs to invest time and effort into building a connection before any sexual involvement. If a man is genuinely interested in you and sees a future together, he will happily wait for months before becoming intimate. This approach helps filter out those guys who are only looking for a casual fling.

When it comes to relationships, many guys are like kids at a piñata party - blindfolded and swinging around, hoping to make a connection. They often lack a clear plan or strategy. Now, don't get me wrong, not every guy is clueless. But let's be honest: many men struggle to understand what women want and when they want it. You also need to know that there are some guys out there who find it challenging to commit, no matter how amazing the woman or connection is.

If you don't take charge, you're simply going along with whatever decisions the guy makes (and, let's be honest, they often choose the easy way out! Not exactly a recipe for success). That's why it's important to understand the frustrating and tricky psychology of men. If you get intimate with a guy too quickly, he might perceive it as moving too fast and start to pull away, feeling like he has nothing to work for. Your body is valuable, so if you give it up too soon and he decides that he doesn't want a relationship, it can leave you feeling down. You may have already noticed this in your past dating experiences or with your friends.

Every person and relationship is unique, so it's hard to make generalisations about what may or may not impact someone's interest in another person. People have different preferences, values, and expectations when it comes to intimacy and dating. It's all about finding someone whose values and desires align with yours. Ultimately, open communication and mutual respect are key in any relationship.

When a man and a woman start sleeping together, it's important to remember that men typically don't form emotional connections just through sex, while we women often do. For the man, it may simply be about the physical aspect, whereas you might start catching feelings and envisioning a future with him before you even really know him if sex happens before you get to know things about him – such as his habits, beliefs, world views, etc. Then, you may find out after you've slept with them that you do not want to date them any longer. On the flip side, you might even find yourself attaching to him before you even get to know if he is a good fit for you.

If you're looking for tips on how to deal with guys and understand their thoughts when it comes to dating, here's some handy advice. Unless the guy you're seeing is excited about taking things further, he's probably just enjoying himself and hasn't given much thought to getting serious. If you're unsure about how a guy feels, it's best to assume he's still figuring things out because, trust me, when that guy is ready, you will know it; you will not be unsure. This way, you'll have the upper hand and won't get your hopes up too high.

The amazing thing is, when you create a chill and stress-free atmosphere, it can make him naturally want to be closer to you, even without realising it. So, just be yourself and enjoy hanging out! Having a relaxed and easy-going vibe has this magical effect that draws guys towards you. It's like they can't help but feel more connected and intrigued by you. I don't know why men work that way, but they just do!

The fact is, even if you have a great connection with a guy, it can take a lot of time spent together before he considers getting serious. He needs to understand the importance of commitment to you. Suppose you believe that constantly smothering him with love, being overly emotional, and being excessively nice, caring, and giving is the key to grabbing a guy's attention. In that case, you may be missing what truly motivates men.

Sometimes, it will be challenging to comprehend what's happening inside his head and what motivates him to desire a long-term relationship. Keeping the spark alive involves more than just engaging in activities that bring you joy; it also entails understanding his perspective and what keeps him engaged.

Just imagine being able to empathise with him while remaining true to yourself.

It would be like having a secret power that makes you incredibly appealing in EVERY aspect of your life. When it comes to attracting and connecting with a man, it's not just about selfish love. It's about how you act, your emotions, and how you communicate with him. Focusing on these aspects can ignite positive feelings and reactions within him, ultimately helping you forge a strong bond.

If you can change your mindset and look at things from a different angle, it will make dealing with men much easier for you. Don't just rely on your OWN way of thinking in these situations.

Think about it...

When women make an effort to do things like cooking, shopping, cleaning, sharing feelings, and nurturing a man, they are doing wonderful and generous things. However, it doesn't necessarily mean that the guy will suddenly become more interested or attracted to her. The things she's doing are probably just things she would want him to do for HER. So, it might not have the desired effect of capturing his attention. You need to consider what HE may appreciate rather than what you would appreciate. This is the secret!

"So, how do I do this?"

Well, my love, the key is to embrace your uniqueness and keep things excitingly unpredictable! Men are naturally drawn to women who can effortlessly blend seriousness and fun in unexpected ways. By keeping them guessing, you'll always leave them pondering about you. When you can playfully keep a guy guessing, it's like sprinkling a touch of magic into the relationship. However, when you add a more serious element to the mix, it creates an irresistible combination that ignites attraction and keeps him captivated. It's the perfect recipe for making him want to stick around.

Picture this: You're out and about, having a great time chatting with an interesting guy at a cool bar or restaurant. Usually, we ladies tend to ask the usual questions about his life, job, and family - you know how it goes! But let's be honest here. That approach is so boring and predictable. Sure, it might work sometimes if you're incredibly lucky or happen to be a drop-dead gorgeous supermodel who turns heads without even saying a word. But for us mere mortals, let's add some excitement into the mix, shall we?

Who wants to be boring and predictable? If you stick to the same old routine, you can't call yourself an interesting person, can you? So, why not add some spice and throw in some unexpected actions? Trust me, life becomes much more thrilling when you do! Talking about mundane stuff can be a real turn-off if you do it too much. It's nice to know some details about someone's life and history, but going overboard with it can push people away.

Why not shake things up and steer the conversation into your unique lane? Keep him guessing by introducing unexpected subjects to chat about or tell funny anecdotes. Don't hesitate to ask some mind-boggling questions that make him think. And don't forget, maintain a flirty vibe and keep eye contact throughout—it's all part of the fun!

"But why should I do this?"

Well, by playfully challenging a man's thoughts and character, you can make a lasting impression on him, and it will make you stand out from the crowd. This sets you apart from the majority of other women who either can't or won't engage in such intellectual banter. So, go ahead and showcase your unique personality! While it's true that sometimes ladies show interest by being overly sweet, flirty, and laughing at every little thing a guy says, it's important to be mindful that this behaviour can sometimes come off as cheesy, exaggerated, and insincere.

Helping guys feel more attracted to you might sometimes mean stepping out of your usual comfort zone. I get how not every woman is cool with the idea of testing or pushing guys a bit. Many think that their personality alone should be enough to draw guys in without any extra work. They see making moves to attract guys or giving them a little challenge, such as playing mind games or messing with them somehow. But hey, it's worth noting that trying new things and stepping outside your comfort zone can lead to personal growth and stronger connections.

"If a relationship is meant to be, it should naturally fall into place without you having to put in much effort, shouldn't it?"

Some people might consider it sneaky to use tactics to catch a guy's attention. Wouldn't it be amazing if your dream man just appeared out of nowhere, exactly when you needed him, and love effortlessly saved the day for a perfect fairy-tale ending? However, if you've been in the dating scene and experienced your fair share of not-so-great relationships, then you probably know that this isn't typically how things work.

I get it if you're a bit hesitant about using certain strategies. But think of it this way: don't we all have our little tricks up our sleeves? Like whipping up a meal even when we're not really into cooking or dressing up for a date? Aren't these just ways to tilt things in our favour? And it's not just us women who do this - plenty of guys have their crafty tactics, too. We've all seen it - fancy dinners or turning up with flowers, all in the hopes of getting a certain response. It's just how the game is played sometimes!

At the end of the day, being in a relationship is all about getting to know each other and figuring out how to make each other smile. Some might see this as playing mind games, while others think it's just real attempts to tighten the bond between two people. No matter what's going on, good old honest talk and staying true to yourself are key to building a healthy and fulfilling relationship.

Okay, now that we're done talking about playing games, let's get straight to the point and discuss what works with men:

CHAPTER

33

"When he pulls away".

*H*ave you ever been in a relationship where everything was going great, and then suddenly, he started to emotionally withdraw just when you were starting to feel comfortable? It can feel like a punch to the gut, can't it? Your first instinct might be to panic, but trust me, freaking out will only make things worse. Emotional outbursts will only push him further away. So, while you may be able to make him pull away, can you also bring him back?

Absolutely, you can! If you chase after a horse in an open field will only cause it to flee further away. Instead, if you ignore it or stop pursuing it, the horse is more likely to approach you. The same principle applies to relationships with men. If a man is genuinely interested, he will make it known.

You know what's interesting? When he pulls away and stops calling, many women find it challenging to control their emotions. As a result, it's common for us to overcompensate by expressing all of our wants and needs to him. It's almost as if we believe that showering him with love and desire will magically make him understand and empathise with us, don't you think? However, that assumption is incorrect.

Let's get straight to the point: understanding what every individual man truly wants is an impossible task. Anyone who claims to have all the answers is either being dishonest or merely sharing their personal perspective. The reality is that every man is unique, and there is no universal answer that applies to all men, so you just have to get to work out your guy and what makes him tick,

"So, why DO guys suddenly pull away for no reason after a short time dating?"

252

Well, this may surprise you, but here goes: Sometimes, guys pull away to test how much we like them or to unintentionally test us. They might give us challenges to see how we handle tough situations and if we can keep our composure. This type of behaviour often occurs in the early stages of dating when they suddenly start to withdraw.

You need to hear this... When faced with a situation where a man starts acting distant or showing disinterest, many women tend to make a common mistake. They may react by saying, "I can't believe you're doing this," or "Is everything ok? Why are you going cold?"

NO, NO, NO!!! Don't do this!!

It is incredibly important not to let him manipulate your emotions by acting distant and moody. He may try to make you doubt yourself, but you need to ask yourself if you want a guy who pulls away when things get tough. Don't fall for it. Take control and make decisions based on logic rather than letting your emotions manipulate you.

"So, what do I do if he pulls away?"

Whether your man is falling in love with you or it's just the early stages of your relationship and you're unsure of his feelings, it can be stressful when he starts pulling away. It doesn't matter how long he pulls away, whether it's a day, a week, or even a month - it still hurts. After all, you've invested your precious time, energy, and emotions into this man.

You need to match his energy! If he pulls, you pull, too. At this stage, it's important to show him that you won't tolerate bad behaviour. Always remember that we are only treated the way we allow ourselves to be treated!

So, for him to pull away from you at any moment, it's painful. As a woman, you would feel that his lack of presence leaves a void that is difficult to fill. Well. Just to clarify, I want to make sure you understand that I'm NOT saying it's okay for a guy to make excuses, keep his distance, and not call or bail on you. That kind of behaviour is a warning sign and shows immaturity, especially if it continues beyond the first few weeks or months.

Sometimes, guys tend to become distant. In such situations, it's important to give them space and allow them to have their own time. Just relax and give it some time. If you stay calm and easy-going, he might come back around. But if he does, you need to make it clear that you won't tolerate this behaviour going forward, and then you need to be grateful that he showed you who he was earlier on in the relationship. You dodged a bullet!

"But why do men do this?"

It could be for numerous reasons. Typically, men are seen as the pursuers in relationships, with women often portrayed as the pursued. So, when a man suddenly becomes distant, it can feel like a power shift is happening. This change can make you feel like you're now the one who needs to chase him and may lead to self-doubt or lowered confidence. This tactic sometimes works, and it might make him seem more valuable in your eyes while also making you less likely to consider other options. It also puts you in a position where your interest level is revealed, flipping the traditional dynamic on its head.

Think of it this way. If you start coming across as too pushy or desperate about the future with a guy, he might get the impression that you're trying to control him or that you're needy and overly reliant on him, and well, that could make him want to stay single. Now, if a guy genuinely believes his life would be better and less complicated by staying single or casually dating, what should he do? Well, I can share some insights based on my own experience with my male clients.

Firstly, to navigate through this situation, it's essential to identify what might be causing him to pull back from you out of the blue. It's evident that things have shifted recently, yet he maintains there's no issue, and his feelings remain unchanged. This denial itself is a concern that needs addressing with kindness and understanding.

Here are a few reasons he might be avoiding this discussion:

- *It appears that he is stressed out about other things. Have you considered other aspects of his life? Could his family or work be causing him stress? It's possible that this situation isn't about you at all but rather about him withdrawing because he's going through something.*

- *He is experiencing confusion regarding his feelings. It is important to understand that feelings are not static; they constantly change and transform. He acknowledges that he is experiencing a shift in his emotions, but he is uncertain about the underlying reasons and how to navigate through them. Therefore, he is taking some time to introspect and gain a better understanding of himself.*

- *He is simply trying to keep things calm. There might be a small issue bothering him, but it's not a big deal. He doesn't want you to overreact or start an argument. He is just figuring out the best way to communicate with you.*

- *He is losing interest.*

It's important for guys to feel independent and free, even when they're in a relationship. This doesn't mean that they want to have intimate time with other women, but rather that they need to feel in control of their own lives, just like you do. However, when the woman they're with constantly pressures them to settle down, their need for independence can quickly turn into restlessness, resentment, and fear.

Do you want a guy to get serious with you because you pressured him or because he genuinely wants to be with you?

Instead of getting all worked up, let's break it down logically: why would he suddenly distance himself?

Answer: He needs space, whether it's physical or emotional.

So, what happens when you fail to respect personal space and keep getting closer to the guy who pulled away? Well, logically, he will pull even further away. And what happens when you chase him? He runs! Why? Because he still needs the space he initially took! It's common sense, isn't it? His need doesn't disappear just because you chased him into a corner.

So, if you don't want to drive him away, just give him some room to breathe. Simple as that. No need for drama, no tears, shouting or sulking. And no interrogations! Just let him do his thing while you get on with your own life. Never forget that your world doesn't revolve around him! You lived perfectly fine before you met him, and you will live perfectly fine without him!

"But what will happen if I give him space?"

Once he has had the time and space, it's important for him to figure himself out. He will appreciate that you were a well-adjusted and confident woman who respected his needs. If he comes back, he will return to you with more confidence in his choice and in himself. He may now be truly ready to commit to you. After taking the time to think about it, he has decided that you are the woman he wants. There are no doubts. This will now be a situation where both of you can feel confident in the relationship.

Now, would you agree that doing this would make you feel a thousand times better about yourself than constantly nagging him to commit and him reluctantly following suit? Who wants to feel like a guy is with them because they nagged them into it?

The worst-case scenario is that he has decided to break up with you, and you know what? That's perfectly fine. Who wants a guy who doesn't want them? His departure should be seen as a blessing because now you have the opportunity to meet the right person for you!

It is a win-win

CHAPTER

34

"Be the girl that makes him commit".

*T*his is the harshest truth, and I am so sorry if you are not ready to hear this, BUT I have to tell you that if a man tells you he has a commitment problem, nine times out of ten, it simply means he has a problem committing to YOU. Look, it's not important why he can't fully commit to you. Whether it's because of relationship problems, things he can't accept about you, or his issues, don't sweat it. What matters is that when you hear something like this, you know exactly what he's saying: "I'm just not that into you..."

Usually, when a guy says he has commitment issues while dating you, he's waiting for something or someone better to show up in his life. If he believes there's someone out there who's even better than you, he won't take the relationship further because he'll think he's settling.

"So, what's a girl to do then?"

I feel like it's one of those "hiding in plain sight" things. We're so desperate to figure out every little thing that we often overlook the obvious solution. It is SIMPLE: Never let yourself be a crutch for a guy's self-delusion, and don't be the kind of woman that a man can keep hanging on forever. If you feel like he thinks he can do better, say bye-bye to that dude. Move on, focus on your personal growth, and aim to date guys who truly see and value your worth in every way.

If you're seeking a serious relationship with a guy, keep in mind that having a strong mental connection can be even more crucial than mere physical attraction. It's the foundation for lasting connections! Physical chemistry may fade over time, but intellectual compatibility is key for forming a deep and lasting connection. By the way, learning important details about him right from the start can help you make wise decisions about your future as a couple.

Never waste your time trying to win over men whose ideal partner doesn't resemble you at all. They are not your target audience. Have faith that the man you're looking for is searching for someone like you. And if he isn't, then he's not the right man for you. Simples!!

Avoid auditioning him. When you're on a date, instead of fretting over whether he's interested in you, flip the script and ask yourself, "Am I interested in him?" If he implies that he'll only stay if you alter certain aspects of yourself, don't fall for it. He's not the right person for you. The ideal partner for a long-lasting relationship will value you exactly as you are – no need for pretending!

You shouldn't have to play mind games or question his intentions. If you're constantly trying to decipher his text messages, it's a sign that he doesn't like you that much. And if you feel like you have to choose the perfect moment to have sex with him, fearing that he'll disappear if you don't get it right, it's another indication that he is not that into you.

The guy who's really into you will be smitten from the get-go. No matter what you do, he won't be put off. It'll be clear as day that he's got a thing for you. But that doesn't mean you should rush things and jump into his bed. There's a sweet spot between being overly affectionate and keeping things mysterious.

Don't fall into the trap of thinking that if you shower a guy with enough affection or do lots for him, he'll feel like he has to stick around. Guys don't care about how much you've given them. If they decide to move on after taking all you've done for him for a decade, they just will. If a guy isn't really into you or doesn't see himself settling down, no amount of love or effort from your side is going to make him stay forever. But if he's really into you, trust me, it won't be so hard work keeping him around!

When it comes to dealing with guys, dating, and relationships, there is much more to consider beyond just words. Body language, tone of voice, and other non-verbal cues associated with social status play a significant role. Being mindful of these subtle details can greatly enhance your interactions and improve your understanding of these situations.

Let's be real here:

If you can tackle the everyday worries and frustrations that women face with a cheeky sense of humour without letting them bring you down, then guess what? You're not just another face in the crowd. You're a shining beacon of awesomeness!

You're an exceptional woman in a man's mind.

CHAPTER
35

"Don't be a doormat."

*F*rom my extensive experience, I'd like to share some sage advice: it's important not to act like a girlfriend to a guy who isn't your boyfriend and isn't offering any commitment. Trust me, many men may happily accept home-cooked meals, cleaning, washing and sex, and he could even let you iron his shirts but still not be ready to commit to you. Please don't let your self-esteem suffer by trying to be useful to a guy in the hopes that he will choose you.

If you find yourself in a relationship where you're being a supportive girlfriend, but your man hasn't shown any signs of including you in his future plans, it's possible that he may be using you as a steppingstone. The same goes if you've been there for him through thick and thin without seeing any growth in the relationship. It might be time to take a step back and reassess your role in his life. Remember, you deserve someone who values and includes you in their future.

Don't just settle for being the woman who helps him succeed but often gets left behind for someone else in the end. This kind of woman is incredibly loyal and supportive, sticking with her man through thick and thin, even if he ends up finding someone else who he considers his 'dream woman'.

I grew up believing that being a "nice and supportive girlfriend" who's always there to help her man with everything was the key to winning his heart. It did not make sense to me that doing anything other than supporting him could keep him attracted and interested. If I saw a woman who was attracted to a mean and abusive guy, I would assume she has some issues or that the guy must be charming at other times.

Unfortunately, many women (myself included in the past) are drawn to men who we think need a "good woman's touch."

But it's crucial to realise that getting involved with these men may not be the wisest decision. Often, you'll find yourself being a stepping stone on their path to success.

No one wants to find themselves in a situation where they stick by their partner's side through thick and thin, only to discover later that their partner never intended to marry them. It's a risky move to invest the best years of your life in a man, hoping that he will eventually propose or commit to you.

How your love life pans out can show if a man is just playing games or if he sees a future with you. Like, imagine you're in your early twenties, and you've been dating your college sweetheart for around a year. It wouldn't be the best idea to expect him to pop the question right before or after graduation, right?

However, if you're in your late twenties and your boyfriend of a year doesn't seem to envision a future with you, it might be time to reconsider things. The same applies to those in their thirties who have been dealing with an indecisive guy for over two years. And if you're hitting your forties and realise that your so-called "Prince Charming" is simply taking advantage of you without any real commitment, well... you know what to do!

If you're looking for something serious like marriage, it's crucial to be clear about your expectations right from the beginning. If you feel like he's hesitating or unsure about taking the next step, don't hesitate to encourage him a little. You deserve someone who appreciates your time and effort, especially if you've been supporting him for a long time.

"So, how can I avoid being in this kind of relationship?"

Well, after observing women persistently making the same mistakes with guys and expecting different outcomes, I had a revelation that completely transformed my perspective on everything.

I quickly realised that when women playfully test and challenge men, it captures the attention of quality men who stick around longer. What is even more surprising is that when a woman clearly communicates her desires to a man, it often works in her favour, as long as she doesn't put too much pressure on him. It may sound strange, but sometimes, being a bit selfish can make men feel drawn to you and more receptive to your ideas.

Isn't it strange? Sarcasm, playing hard to get, challenging their beliefs and actions, and other "illogical" things like telling a guy that you will only seriously date him if he's open to considering marriage in the future work when it comes to attracting and keeping good men... It is important to realise that setting boundaries with men has many positive benefits beyond just "being nice." If you are always being nice and experiencing negative consequences, it's likely affecting your self-esteem.

Believe me, those who genuinely care for you will always stand by your side, regardless of the circumstances. However, be prepared that your blossoming self-assurance might not sit well with everyone - and that's perfectly fine. This shift will function as a test to distinguish between your real love and those who might be exploiting you. Do not let their adverse reactions shake your confidence - remember, it's their issue to deal with, not yours.

You can be assertive and still be nice. You can be strong for yourself while maintaining respectful relationships. I love witnessing people discover how to communicate effectively on their own. It's empowering and can truly change your life for the better.

CHAPTER

36

"Attraction is not a choice".

*S*o, why are guys seemingly drawn to selfish women or "bitches"? Well, the simple truth is that it's not a conscious decision for them; it just sort of happens naturally.

Attraction and emotions are not always under our conscious control. Men do not intentionally choose to feel attracted to selfish women, just as you do not choose to feel drawn to unavailable men. It's important to remember that emotions and attraction can be complex and confusing.

Nature has wired men and women with different attraction mechanisms. Women's attraction tends to be more intricate, while men often find themselves effortlessly drawn to a good-looking woman. However, let's not overlook the fact that women are also attracted to attractive men. But, let's be honest, for us, it's not all about looks. In fact, we women are often more interested in certain personality traits and behaviours rather than just a handsome face.

"So, what exactly attracts men intellectually to "selfish" women?"

Well, let me be upfront and clear about what it's NOT: It's not a lack of generosity on their part. I believe that women who display the kind of selfishness I'm referring to are not necessarily lacking in generosity when it comes to their emotions, possessions, and so on. Most men are not into abusive, mean, or negative women. In fact, healthy guys steer clear of toxic personalities. Let's talk about those women who are often seen as selfish but still manage to have a certain charm that men find irresistible.

Men often rationalise and excuse negative behaviour because they are highly attracted to other qualities.

Get ready for a sneak peek at some factors that grab a man's attention and make him fall head over heels. These are the ingredients for pure magic:

- *Unpredictability.*
- *Uncontrollability.*
- *Challenging.*
- *Casual Interplay of Dominance/Submission.*

When presented correctly, the qualities I've listed above can activate the natural attraction mechanism in men. However, some women who display "bitchy" behaviour may have taken these naturally attractive qualities to an extreme. Despite their presence, these qualities still possess the power to trigger attraction.

Now, let's break it down. What does all of this mean for you? It's simple. You can be a decent person and STILL attract the attention of men. The key here is to enhance your flirting skills and gain confidence in engaging with them. The key is to discover your own personal style and stay true to yourself and your own boundaries.

In the end, you'll find that this approach can help you achieve your goals while maintaining your standards when dealing with men. It also means you won't have to be the go-to person for relationship advice or listen to others complain about their demanding partners. You have the power to be the woman they date and enjoy quality time with. Embrace it! Take a moment to think about how you can incorporate those four qualities I mentioned earlier into your own unique personality.

It's about bringing out your best self and leaving a lasting impression.

Why not inject some excitement into your life and embrace spontaneity? Don't allow external factors or other people to dictate every aspect of your life. Be assertive and show the world that you are not someone to be underestimated. Take a moment to connect with your assertive and confident side (and let's be clear, I mean confident, not pushy). It's also worth considering the advantages that come from being both generous and looking out for yourself simultaneously.

Oftentimes, the notion of being selfish is frowned upon. However, allow me to shed some light on this - it's not always a negative trait! It's about articulating your needs and desires effectively without coming across as too forceful or demanding. It's about fostering open and honest dialogue whilst also honouring others' boundaries rather than imposing your own wishes upon them. So, you see, a touch of 'selfishness' can actually be quite beneficial!

CHAPTER 37

"Never be needy".

*L*et me address the topic of neediness and insecurity directly…

The majority of men I talk to find neediness and insecurity unappealing in the context of dating. These characteristics, although not immediately apparent to some women, are often considered significant deterrents for men in the dating world. A woman who lacks self-assurance feels doubtful about her actions, or perceives a man's behaviour as potentially harmful may unintentionally project an image of being needy and insecure. It is important to acknowledge that everyone experiences these feelings at various stages in their lives.

I've been there myself; I will not lie…

Allowing insecurities to take control and seeking validation solely from a man or a relationship is akin to relying solely on money for genuine happiness. It simply won't suffice. While it may provide a temporary surge of excitement and alter your immediate circumstances and emotions, let's be honest; in the grand scheme of things, it won't truly transform your sense of self.

"Can being too needy and insecure actually drive your guy away?"

Well, it's no secret that men have a knack for picking up on clingy and insecure behaviour. At no time should a man come into your life and be the "be-all and end-all." You should NEVER cancel out your friends, family, and your own hobbies and interests for this guy. Of course, when the dopamine hits, you want your fix! The feelings when you're with this guy are out of control! It's amazing! BUT STOP!

Men value what they have to work for (yes, I have written this yet again, but it is THAT important!). So, don't stop living your life and become "Little Miss Always Available." Don't give up your passion for this new guy. Stay busy with your Zumba classes, studying, writing that new thriller you've always wanted to, or tending your tomato plants - whatever brings you joy! Don't let this new guy come in and demand all your time. And, most importantly, don't let him come before your tomatoes! He will appreciate the time he gets with you, and he'll have to put in the EFFORT to make plans with you. Trust me on that one.

You know, it's funny how sometimes, without even a wink of awareness, your choice of words or body language can send out a little SOS signal to the guys. It's like you're wearing a neon sign that says "needy" or "insecure". And once a guy gets that image in his head, well, darling, it sticks like gum on a shoe. It can really put a different spin on how he pictures any future with you.

When a guy notices clingy behaviour in a girl, it tends to colour his view of her. It's as if this neediness becomes the lens through which he sees their hangouts - from casual meetups to more intimate times. Let's be real here: nothing kills a guy's interest faster.

Let's look at a few examples of people displaying neediness and insecurity:

Excessively holding onto or touching a man.

You know, when we're out and about, too much touchy-feely can sometimes come off as a bit clingy. If you find yourself always being the one to initiate physical contact, he might begin to feel a tad smothered by it all. Now, don't get me wrong - there's nothing wrong with wanting to reach out and touch him. But remember, less is often more. Try going for those quick, unexpected moments that will catch him off guard and leave a lasting impression.

Speaking negatively about other women.

Ever found yourself resorting to name-calling other women, using words like "slut," "bitch," or "crazy"? It's something that happens when we feel threatened or insecure, especially when someone attractive comes into the picture or if there's a woman catching our guy's eye. But here's the thing: this kind of talk doesn't really win any points with men. They see it as a cover-up for our own insecurities and a constant need for validation and attention. The real secret? We need confidence in ourselves without needing anyone else's opinion to validate us.

Being mean about previous partners.

You know, constantly badmouthing previous relationships can work against us. It might unintentionally sendoff vibes that we're feeling insecure or dealing with some emotional stuff. It's not always easy to see it ourselves, right? These actions could also hint at past relationship hiccups - and let's be honest, those can be a real handful to deal with.

Acting overly emotional.

If a man notices that you are easily rattled, upset, or frustrated, he may perceive you as insecure and assume that you will treat him the same way. This could potentially scare him away from you.

Trying too hard for attention.

When women try to act overly sexy, funny, cool, or smart, they often end up looking foolish, which can give the impression that they are not comfortable with themselves, according to men's perception. But here's a tip: DON'T DO IT! If you possess any of these qualities, he will notice you in a negative way. The best approach to getting noticed is to be subtle and suggestive.

Creating drama.

Hey there, we all have those moments, don't we? Sometimes, as women, we might find ourselves making a mountain out of a molehill. We get caught up in disagreements or heighten conflicts over things that might not be that significant. When this happens, and a man sees us getting upset over small matters, it could give off vibes of insecurity.

CHAPTER

38

"Get your date on".

*H*ere's a thought for you: Why not step out of your comfort zone and start exploring relationships with different men? It could be an exciting journey to discover the one who truly complements you. And guess what? There's something to be said about taking your time and not rushing into physical intimacy. This isn't just about playing hard to get; think of it like marinating a steak … give it some time, and you might just be pleasantly surprised by the juicy rewards that await!

Taking this path could be just the thing to hone your intuition and bring a sense of calm as you navigate the dating landscape. It's all about personal growth and broadening your horizons. Yes, it might feel a bit unconventional, but playing the field could actually up your charm game! So why not take the plunge and relish in the adventure? Just remember to stay transparent and truthful – laying down ground rules is crucial to prevent getting overly entangled with your suitors.

By gently hinting that you're open to exploring other relationships and taking charge of your decisions, you're setting a powerful tone about the kind of relationship you deserve. Any man who wants to be with you must rise to these standards before you even think about committing to him.

"But won't that put him off me?"

No way! It's funny how things work out sometimes. When a guy realises he can't just snap his fingers and have you, it creates a mix of respect and longing. It may sound strange, but that's life for you! If you play the dating game like this, don't be surprised if men who didn't pay you much attention before suddenly start taking notice. And remember what I said about men always wanting more? It turns out to be true! Guys who date frequently often have an advantage in finding the right partner.

These men have dedicated a significant amount of time to find their perfect match. Along the journey, they have encountered a few obstacles, but they have discovered what truly matters to them in a relationship.

Let me put it this way … If you're actively seeking a partner without a clear idea of what you want, chances are you might end up with someone simply because he is the only one showing interest in you at that moment. However, it's important to be realistic and acknowledge that just because someone is attracted to you and showing interest, it doesn't necessarily mean they are your forever person.

Let's look a little bit deeper into your potential dream guy on paper. Think about his personality traits: Is he laid-back, energetic, caring, inspiring, sensitive, or maybe even a bit rugged?

Write down all the traits that come to mind …

- What are his greatest enjoyments? What does he value most? (Is it intelligence, physical prowess, money, family, freedom...)
- How does he treat and interact with the people around him, including his family, friends, and exes?
- Where is he in his professional life?
- How does he physically interact with you?
- What is his dating history?
- Where does he see himself in the future?
- Here is some space to write it:

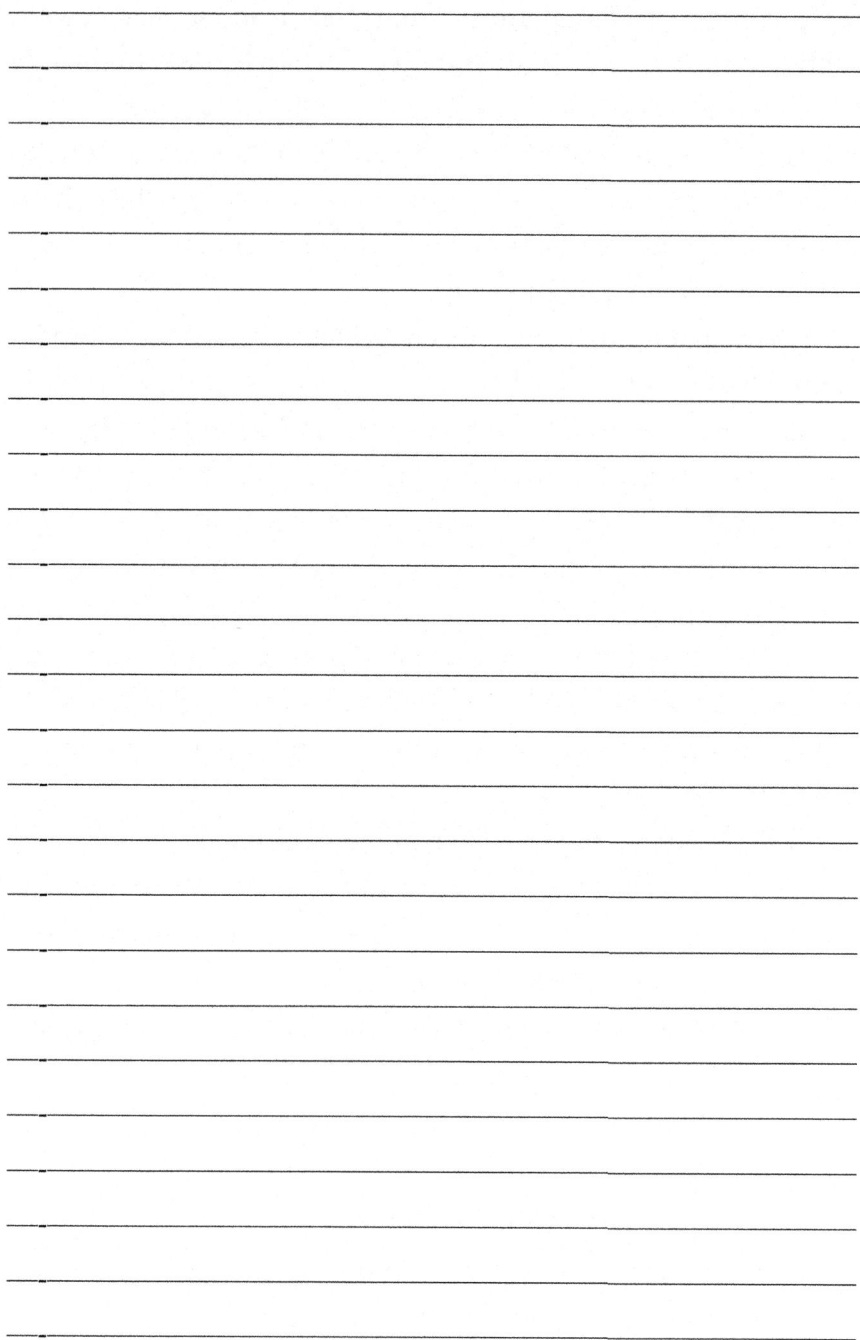

When you fill in the answers here with no shame in your game, you're connecting with your own honest expectations about the type of man you would like to be with. If you get involved with a guy without clearly setting your expectations, it's like following a recipe for disappointment and annoyance and then wondering why you end up feeling disappointed and annoyed. It's crucial to acknowledge and voice your expectations, even if they are just in your own mind so that when you bump into him, you recognise him!

Don't hold back on your expectations, and never underestimate yourself. We're talking about your future here, as well as matters of the heart and your love life. Taking the time to write down your answers is not just about clarifying your expectations, but it also helps solidify your beliefs and desires in your mind. By doing so, you'll start seeing them as non-negotiable requirements in a partner, setting higher standards for better things to come.

You might find it hard to believe, but the more you contemplate these ideas, the more they manifest as reality in your life. It's all about how your thoughts and beliefs shape your experiences.

I need you to know that the choices you make now can greatly affect your future love life, especially if this guy happens to be "the one." The way you attract guys can say a lot about your personality and what you're seeking. It's normal to enjoy some attention, isn't it? However, constantly seeking a guy's attention can make you appear clingy or insecure. And let's be honest, these traits don't exactly contribute to building a strong and appealing relationship.

You know what I've noticed? Sometimes, women overlook the importance of those little things - the small interactions, body language, tone of voice, and even the tiniest hints of attitude that they bring to the table. Every little thing you do contributes to your overall behaviour. Each individual action, no matter how small, plays a vital role in shaping who you are as a person. So, don't underestimate the significance of even the tiniest details in creating the bigger picture.

And that leads me to one of the biggest mistakes you can make with men when you first meet them...

CHAPTER

39

"Don't give up the goods too quickly."

While I am a supporter of any woman who is completely at ease jumping between the sheets without any strings attached, after all, we all have needs … been there, done that; I have to say that there's also a good number of women that I have coached who end up feeling very upset and hurt when these steamy encounters don't blossom into something more committed. This is when you must think about your short-term goals with the guys or your long-term goals.

It seems that men have a little secret that could greatly enhance their chances of committing to a long-term relationship if us women were aware of it.

Surprisingly, guys tend to keep this secret hidden because they fear that if women find out, they might have to put in more effort. When a guy sees a woman as a potential long-term partner, he may be willing to be patient in certain areas, like intimacy. Allow me to explain this in simpler terms…

MAKE THAT MAN WAIT FOR THE GOODIES!!!

Before engaging in a sexual relationship with a man, YOU typically hold most of the power in the dynamic. However, after getting intimate, your influence may diminish significantly. So, if your goal is a long-term relationship or even marriage, it's not advisable to relinquish all your power to casual flings. Here's the thing: guys are more likely to lose interest if they can have all the fun without putting in any effort. It's like the saying goes, "Why buy the cow when you can get the milk for free?"

It's crucial to remember that guys genuinely appreciate the sacrifices they make to achieve something; they want to win the prize. As I mentioned before, a guy's actions towards you reflect how much he cares about you and how he sees you. The more he invests his time plans significant dates for you, and commits to your relationship, the more difficult it is for him to downplay your importance, even if things don't work out in the end.

It's interesting to see that the more a guy is invested in a relationship, the higher the likelihood of maintaining his long-term interest.

But here's the most important part: it's not just about outdated ideas that women shouldn't sleep with men. It's because women naturally tend to get emotionally attached to a guy when they have sex with him - it's just part of our DNA. The key reason to hold off on jumping into bed with a guy is that you need to truly get to know who he is as a person beyond just physical attraction. This is a common reason why many relationships fail - when they're solely built on great sex rather than true compatibility with the person.

I mean, whilst steamy sex is great, ultimately, a relationship is a friendship with extras. So, you need to make sure that this person could potentially be your best friend. Otherwise, you are just going to end up in another dead-end relationship as soon as the honeymoon period is over.

You see when you refuse to settle for being just another woman in his life, he has no choice but to recognise your worth. Some women may not even realise that constantly hooking up with men who aren't seeking commitment can seriously damage their self-confidence over time. It's like a punch in the gut every time a guy disappears after becoming intimate. This is especially tough when all you truly desire is a genuine relationship.

Here's another harsh truth: **Certain men will say just about anything to get you naked!**

Isn't it baffling how a guy who might seem pretty ordinary can suddenly turn into a strategic genius when it comes to winning over a woman? It's downright exasperating when the same man who used to shower you with texts, ditch his friends just to spend time with you and surprise you at work with sweet gestures can vanish like Houdini as soon as things get intimate!

You know, when it comes to intimacy in a relationship, we women have quite a bit of influence. We're the ones who decide when to take that next step, which is a pretty big deal in any relationship. But here's the thing: once we've shared that intimate moment with our partner, we've lost some of our leverage because we've already shown our cards. Sure, you could choose to stop being intimate if he starts losing interest, but since he's already experienced what he was after, it might not make as much of an impact on him as you'd hope.

Have you ever noticed a common thread among the men you've encountered, even those who might come across as players? It's quite fascinating. They all share a similar experience with the women they end up getting serious with. These women have a unique approach - they insist on slowing things down, focusing on building an authentic bond and deeper intimacy before moving into the physical realm.

"Just how slow are we talking about?"

You know, it's a bit like asking how long a piece of string is. The time it takes really varies from person to person. The aim here isn't to manipulate or trick him into a relationship. Instead, the waiting period is all about truly getting to know the man beyond just physical attraction. It's about taking your time to find out what you both have in common, understanding his intentions (is he even interested in a relationship?), figuring out if he's the right one for you and checking if he has the qualities you're looking for. Jumping into intimacy too soon can sometimes blur your judgment on these crucial matters.

Holding off on physical intimacy can be a crucial step if you're aiming for a serious, long-term relationship. Now, I know what you're thinking - we all know that one couple who got intimate on their first date and are now happily married with a house full of kids. But remember, they're more the exception than the rule.

The truth is if you meet a guy that you really like and he likes you back, and he's looking for more than just a quick fling, jumping into bed with him too quickly could make him reconsider and go back to just wanting a fling. When a guy is ready for something more meaningful, he tends to take his time and be patient when it comes to getting physical because there's a deeper connection involved. However, if a guy is only focused on a girl's appearance, patience quickly goes out the window.

I've noticed time and time again, that when a man sees the potential for a lasting relationship, he's willing to patiently wait for the woman and eagerly embrace the opportunity to get to know her better. This is because, when he has to wait, he dedicates his time to genuinely understand and appreciate every aspect of the relationship, getting to know the girl and all about her. He sincerely longs for a deeper connection, which ultimately aligns with what you desire, doesn't it?

Another universal truth you need to know is that by making him wait at the beginning of a long-term relationship, he will respect and trust you more should you end up together in a long-term relationship or a marriage. He will know that you have high standards and are not the type to jump into bed with just anybody so when you are not with him, he will not doubt you. This will elevate your relationship in every possible way.

It's important to understand that men and women may have different approaches when it comes to relationships. Some men may prioritise physical intimacy over deeper emotional connections. However, if a man sees you solely as an object of desire, he may prioritise sex and lack the patience to truly get to know you and build a meaningful connection.

"But what if he gets annoyed from having to wait?"

WHOA!! Don't ignore this warning sign, as it reveals a lot about his intentions! Instead, focus on his actions rather than just his words.

However, even if we have reservations or feel things are moving too quickly, we still end up getting intimate. Afterwards, it can be challenging to change course, and we may start developing emotional connections. We may interpret this as a sign of long-term commitment. However, it's important to remember that not all men view physical intimacy in the same way and may not see it as a sign of a serious relationship.

You know, it's very important to remember that creating a relationship with depth and substance isn't an overnight job. It takes time, patience, and a whole lot of effort. Just focusing on the physical aspect of things won't get you very far in the long run. Sure, sex can be exciting at first, but as time passes by, its appeal can fade.

Ever noticed how a whirlwind romance can sometimes fizzle out just as quickly? When things get physical too soon, it's not uncommon for guys to lose interest and shy away from committing to a long-term relationship. It's like skipping the main course and going straight for dessert; it might seem exciting at first, but eventually, you'll start craving something more substantial. This haste could unintentionally give off vibes of desperation or neediness. And let's be honest, no one wants to feel like they're just another notch on the bedpost. It may seem old-fashioned, but respect still plays a huge role in modern relationships.

As a result of jumping into bed too fast before you get to know him better, the initial spark may begin to fade, causing the guy to hold back or distance himself. This scenario is pretty common—I mean, I hear about it virtually every day in my line of work. Trust me.

To a man, there's something incredibly appealing about a woman who knows her worth. A woman who can firmly uphold her boundaries, yet still make a man feel desired and valued. It's that irresistible combination of strength and allure that men find so captivating.

For example, picture yourself in a passionate moment with him after a great date. Things are heating up, and it's all very exciting. But then you decide to pause and say, "Even though I'm incredibly attracted to you right now, I won't be jumping into bed with you until I know you better." It's so important to combine self-respect with showing a guy that it's okay for him to have sexual desire for you. By doing this, your denial can make him even more attracted to you rather than registering in his head as a rejection.

Remember, simply denying a guy sex isn't what makes him chase you more. If he sees that you require other qualities and emotional investment from him to keep you interested, he'll know that you're a woman of high value who won't be available at his beck and call. And trust me, that is super sexy to men. They all want a woman that no guy can get.

To put it simply, what keeps a man interested in you for more than just a fleeting moment isn't just about intimacy. It's about him seeing you in your element, doing what makes you happiest, and never compromising your standards just because of your feelings for him.

If you're looking to take things to the next level, consider making him wait. If he is truly committed and ready, delaying a bit longer can increase the chances of future success and decrease the likelihood of being ghosted; plus, the better you get to know him, the more you can work out if he is the guy for you.

Just think about spending a little more time stoking the flames of attraction before diving headfirst into a serious relationship. Trust me, it's like marinating your favourite steak; the longer you let it soak, the tastier it gets! When you invest time in building that connection and nurturing his long-term desires for you, your odds of painting a beautiful future together skyrocket.

Now, when we talk about setting standards in relationships, you must remember that no two men are exactly alike! But one thing must stay the same and that is your boundaries. I know I keep mentioning these pesky boundaries – but that is because they are SO important! If you're looking to improve your dating life, I have a hard truth for you: lacking firm boundaries may prevent you from attracting quality men.

Contrary to what you may have heard, men are turned on and attracted to women who have firm boundaries. While they may not openly admit it, firm boundaries also indicate that it may be harder to get you in the sack, which, in turn, makes you more valuable in their eyes, just like those shoes I mentioned earlier!

Girl, make him work for it ... The easier you are to get into bed, the less he will appreciate what he has got!

Boundaries are about you, not other people. They help define who you are and what you're comfortable with. They ensure that you know what you will and won't tolerate from anyone. Boundaries also help you identify problems and find ways to address them. Occasionally, someone may unintentionally cross your boundaries, but that's when you communicate with them. How they react will determine the level of respect they deserve from you.

You know, setting your boundaries and sticking to them is a real show of strength. It's not about being stubborn or unyielding but rather demonstrating that you're not someone who can be easily pushed around or always putting others' happiness before your own. That's a sign of true assertiveness, and it's something to be proud of! By standing firm, upholding your values and refusing to accept anything less than what you deserve, you're broadcasting a potent message: You know your worth and the unique attributes you bring to any situation.

You know, men have this uncanny ability to pick up on inauthenticity, neediness, and a lack of boundaries. It's like they have a sixth sense for it! And once they do catch onto these things, the possibility of a serious relationship often slips away.

Imagine this: you're a woman who has built strong boundaries. Not only does your life take a turn for the better, but you also start attracting the kind of guys you've always wanted. Because, let's face it, the good ones are drawn to women who know their value. And guess what plays a big part in whether a guy is ready to commit? Emotional maturity! I'm not just throwing words around here – I truly believe it! If you want your love story to stand the test of time, building that deep emotional bond with your man is key.

Why? Well, let's be honest, becoming emotionally mature enough to take responsibility for your actions and learn from your mistakes is no walk in the park. Once you start owning your emotions and perspective on life, without blaming others (yes, even men), something truly amazing happens. You'll find a special sense of balance and contentment that is completely yours.

"But tell me, what is the difference between a request and a boundary?"

Well, think of setting boundaries as crafting your personal guidebook to maintain your balance. It's all about standing firm and protecting yourself from those who might not truly care for your well-being. Keep in mind that boundaries aren't about manipulating others; they're purely about taking the reins of your own life.

Consider this: When you say, "Please don't call me", it's not just about setting a boundary; it's also a plea. Let's face it: it can be interpreted as trying to steer the situation. However, if you establish the boundary by saying, "I won't answer when you call," now that's more like it. It centres around you and what you're prepared to put up with. Always remember that maintaining your control is crucial!

Setting emotional boundaries is a very important step towards ensuring our overall well-being. These boundaries act as shields, keeping negativity at bay and nurturing a positive environment for personal growth. And guess what? They can also be quite appealing to others, particularly men. Your confidence and ability to set boundaries might pique their interest, even if they can't exactly put their finger on why.

Emotional fitness is not just a casual stroll; it is the ultimate destination. It is actually quite amusing how there are always people who strongly resist the idea of introspection and personal growth, especially when it has an impact on those around them.

Don't we all secretly wish for a magic guide that could instantly turn men into our dream partners? But, alas, reality doesn't always play out as we'd like. The fact you're here, reading this, is a testament to your determination to enhance your romantic relationships with men – and that's truly admirable! It shows you're open to learning, evolving and welcoming change. By the way, high five to you for taking such an active role in seeking the love you deserve!

However, this is a rule that I believe is worth mentioning, so please pay attention...

GET IN HIS HEAD BEFORE YOU GET IN HIS BEAD!

CHAPTER

40

"Say what you mean".

$\mathcal{J}$f you don't want to casually date forever, it's important to let a man know right from the start! Don't be afraid to be upfront and honest about your intentions. In fact, it can greatly influence how guys perceive you. Being clear about what you want not only shows confidence but also increases the chances of finding someone who has the same relationship goals as you. It also helps filter out those who aren't on the same page as you.

When a woman is upfront about her desires from the start, it can have a significant impact on how a guy sees her. It definitely increases the chances of him being interested in a future together. It also makes him see you as a serious option rather than just a short-term fling. When it comes to relationships, why waste time beating around the bush? Instead, be upfront and set the stage for something truly amazing.

Here's exactly how to do it:

When talking to the guy, you can start by saying something like this: "I have to be upfront with you; I'm not interested in casual relationships. I'm not a woman who is into hook-ups and one-night stands". When you communicate your expectations like this, it subconsciously makes him think, "Wow, this woman is someone I need to respect." Oh, and the best bit is that if he only wants a one-night stand or an easy hookup, he will show his cards in his reaction, and you have dodged a bullet!

You know what you want and can make your own decisions about your life and relationships with men, so he will realise he needs to step up. It's important to convey that you're not easy to get with and have respect for yourself. I can't stress enough how important this is!

When you engage in a genuine conversation with a guy, it has the potential to bring you closer together and make him realise how much he values you compared to how you value yourself. It's all about setting your standards and ensuring that you receive what you truly deserve. If you resist or react negatively when discussing your love life with him, it can make it harder for both of you to move forward and strengthen your bond. So, try approaching these conversations with an open mind and a positive attitude; it will make a significant difference!

If you're trying to build a relationship, it's crucial to avoid making the mistakes of assuming, arguing, begging, convincing, or trying to bully someone into a commitment. Long-term success in relationships relies on approaching them with honesty and respect rather than resorting to manipulative tactics. While it may feel like a victory when someone gives in to your desires immediately, the truth is that there will be significant consequences in the future. When you're ready to take your relationship to the next level, they may not be there for you. So, it's important to consider the long-term impact before pushing for what you want at the moment.

But here's the catch, in order to effectively communicate with him, you need to adapt your own communication style. Sorry, but achieving significant results in life often requires taking the initiative to make them happen. It's an incredible and empowering realisation. No matter how close you believe you are to him, if both of you have a romantic interest, there's a chance that your communication may not be as honest and comfortable as it could be.

Both of you want to express your thoughts accurately, but preconceived notions about each other are influencing how you perceive things. The truth is both of you need to openly communicate your genuine desires and intentions. If you're not on the same page, you'll never be able to harmonise effectively. Poor communication is often blamed for relationship failures. Many men struggle to be completely honest about their intentions and desires due to fears and inhibitions.

CHAPTER
41

"Burned from past heartbreak".

"What if I meet a guy and it doesn't work out?"

*CA*ll right, let's take a moment to explore the darker side of dating. When you choose to enter a new relationship, there is a risk involved in the possibility of you ending up with a broken heart or you are breaking someone else's heart.

Here is an email I received from a client. I have permission to share it, but I will not disclose their name.

I have been single for 4 years by choice, and I have fearlessly guarded my heart. Finding happiness and peace in staying single, I eliminate the risk of having my heart shattered. Falling in love is something I will never allow myself to do again, as I am completely over it.

My current desire is to live a peaceful life devoid of drama, heartbreak, vulnerability, mistreatment, and abuse. I have generalised all men into the same category, believing that they are all manipulative and deceitful rats; even those who may seem good and kind get tarred with the same brush.

I guess I'm too scared to fall in love again. What should I do?

In my response to my client, I emphasised the importance of acknowledging that love can be frightening. It is completely understandable to feel afraid, especially considering past heartbreak. Taking a moment to think differently about it would not betray your heart but rather show compassion towards yourself.

Love is akin to an addiction, offering a euphoric boost that we constantly yearn for, always in search of more to fulfil our emotional needs. However, it can also be painful, as the intensity of love corresponds to the heartache felt during a potential breakup.

Love asks us to open our hearts again and again.

So, where does that leave us? Should we give up on the game called love? Perhaps the answer is yes, at least for a while, until we do the inner work and heal. We need to get over the pain and work through the emotions before we can move on.

I hate to break it to you, but life is finite, and we only have a limited number of years on this planet. So, if you come across someone who shows significant red flags, it's important not to waste your time. Learn to walk away as soon as you identify deal breakers or red flags. Not only will this boost your self-esteem, but more importantly, it will eliminate people who are likely to cause you pain in the future. It's a win-win situation.

It's crucial, however, not to isolate yourself or condemn yourself to a lifetime of being single as a way to protect yourself from potential heartbreak or future hurt. By doing this, you would only harm yourself. Don't be afraid to laugh, love, and have faith in your own intuition. By doing so, you will discover the immense beauty of love and life. Love is an extraordinary experience that has the power to transform your life. Give love another chance, even if you have been hurt before. Be brave!

Love is essentially a lesson in learning how to care for one another. As human beings, we have developed various degrees of addiction to it, affecting us all. Therefore, it is crucial to approach love with the understanding that it begins with self-love. When you prioritise self-love, you are less likely to engage in actions that later cause fear and guilt.

It all stems from a lack of self-trust in relationships. We fear love because we worry about getting hurt. We fear love because we convince ourselves that our partner's choices can shatter the emotional promises we've made. As humans, we often make commitments to ourselves and convince ourselves that our emotions are aligned with those commitments. Memories don't cause pain. Love itself doesn't cause pain. It is the attachment and the expectations that bring the hurt. It is the shattered image of the future we had imagined that causes the pain.

Do you see how relationships can quickly become all about you and how you tend to prioritise yourself while in the midst of them?

Love needs love. That's it.

Love that claims to need anything else is simply personal desire. Personal desires are not inherently wrong, but we must be careful not to confuse them with love, as it can lead to confusion.

I guess I am simply taking a long route to express that if you lack self-trust, which may be a result of past relationships where you were given valid reasons not to trust or you trusted someone who let you down, it is crucial to build trust in yourself. You need to have faith in your own ability to discern whether someone is worth trusting and to stand up for your own needs in a relationship. Trust that no matter what happens, you will be able to cope and thrive.

"But why should I risk the pain of heartbreak again?"

My darling, love is indeed a risk, just like crossing the road. But we don't confine ourselves to our homes 24/7 out of fear, do we? When we open our hearts, we expose ourselves to the possibility of getting hurt, and that's a fact we can't deny. Even if you've experienced heartbreak in the past and feel hesitant about facing that pain again, do not let fear stop you from embracing the opportunity for love in the future.

Take some time for yourself and prioritise your own well-being. Know that regardless of the outcome of a new relationship, you are strong enough to cope with it. Avoid wasting your energy chasing after someone who is not putting in any effort with you. Instead, use this opportunity to reflect, heal, and embrace the next phase of your life. Remember, YOU are the prize, and don't you forget that. You deserve someone who will stand by your side through it all, so don't settle for anything less.

"But what if I just fancy a one-night stand?"

Girl, if you need your itch scratched, go out and get it. I support you 100% as long as you're being safe. But just be aware that you are putting yourself at risk for heartbreak. You may tell yourself it's only sex. And hey, maybe it is! But the bottom line is that your body is your temple, and you deserve to be treated with dignity. Also, as I mentioned before, women often form emotional connections with a guy after being intimate—it's just part of who we are, so be aware!

Even if you're only interested in casual sex, it's important to ensure that you're not putting yourself at risk for any potential disasters. Whether you have feelings for the guy in question or not, it doesn't feel good to be ignored after you've just opened up to someone. No matter how much you tell yourself it's ok, rejection is horrid!

Do you remember how you felt the last time you slept with a guy and he ghosted you? It wasn't a good feeling, was it? That's why I will always encourage you to prioritise taking care of both your heart and your body. It is important to protect yourself emotionally and physically. You are amazing, and your awesomeness deserves to be acknowledged with a follow-up.

The major issue I see is when individuals pursue relationships that they know from the beginning do not align with their goals and values, yet they choose to stay in them for years. It is important to recognise and know when to wave the frogs goodbye. Loneliness should not deceive you into settling for a relationship that is not long-term if that is what you truly desire.

Furthermore, if a guy goes out with you a couple of times and then suddenly disappears (it happens), don't make excuses for him, and don't beat yourself up over it. One of the primary reasons why men disappear after a hook-up is often because they never see you as anything more than a casual encounter right from the start. However, their immaturity prevented them from being honest about their intentions.

If you happen to get ghosted, it's important not to take it personally.Redirect your energy back into yourself. Smile to yourself and realise, you dodged a bullet... chalk it up to experience.

In the future, should you choose to become intimate with a guy, prioritise your own well-being and safety. Make sure that the man you are considering sleeping with respects and values you before you take that step. To put it bluntly: only put yourself in situations that align with your values and make you feel confident in your decisions and your ability to deal with any outcome.

CHAPTER 42

"Do not be scared to be single".

his needs to be mentioned: one of the biggest reasons why so many relationships fail is because people do not know who they want to be with. They don't take the time to figure out what their perfect partner would be like. But most importantly, they jump into a relationship because they are simply lonely or scared to be alone.

The fear of being single or feeling unloved is one of the main reasons why people often settle for the wrong person. In their minds, they believe that having someone, even if it's not the right fit, is better than being alone. However, this mindset can lead to disaster, misery, and heartache. I witness this unfortunate reality almost every day at work.

There is something far worse than being single: being with the wrong person. If I'm honest, the loneliest and most miserable times in my life have occurred when I've been in a relationship with the wrong person. Nothing is lonelier than being in a couple but feeling uncared for and unloved or just knowing that you do not even want to be with that man.

Many years ago, I was with someone on holiday in a beautiful country. As we walked along the beach, I suddenly burst into tears because our relationship was not going well, and he did not make me feel safe. He had a temper that could flare up at any minute and I was so far from home. I felt incredibly lonely. That day, I realised that I would never stay in a wrong relationship again (and I never have).

Feeling unlovable and unattractive leads you to believe that nobody will ever want or love you. However, the truth is that if you don't learn to love yourself, how can you expect others to love you? It's crucial to find happiness in your own company, as it becomes a superpower that radiates self-confidence and attracts others towards you, my darling!

Let me put it this way: if you are content in your own company, confident, and independent, then when you do meet someone, and things don't work out, that's perfectly fine because you know you'll be okay on your own. So, ultimately, this also reduces the likelihood of settling for just any guy out of desperation because you have that inner strength and know that you'll be fine no matter what. You were fine before he came into your life, and you will be fine after. Trust me, it's a powerful mindset to have.

Women who feel down on themselves often fall into the trap of believing they will never meet someone. They may think there are no decent men out there and that no one would want them. They might even feel like they are destined to be single and lonely forever.

Having a negative mindset can easily become a self-fulfilling prophecy. It not only affects your own vibe but also how others perceive you, including guys. That's why it's crucial to cultivate an abundance mindset filled with positivity and confidence. I cannot stress enough how important this is for your overall well-being.

Also, remember that if you have a negative mindset about yourself and doubt the potential of getting into a relationship, you are more likely to find yourself in a rebound situation where you settle for just anybody. This is how some people end up with abusive and uncaring partners.

In my line of work, I have spoken to many women who feel like they are losers if they are not in a relationship; they feel embarrassed going out and being the only single one. But trust me when I tell you, you are a truly special person if you can wait for the right person instead of settling out of fear or insecurity. People will never look down on you for that; in fact, they will admire you for not settling for less than you deserve.

There are many couples out there who are currently unhappy in their relationships and stay together for all the wrong reasons. They sit there and dream of living a lifestyle like the one you might be living right now – free, confident, and not stuck in a dead-end relationship with someone they don't even like.

Let's also talk about the biological clock that kicks in if you haven't had children, which is something you truly desire. It can make you more inclined to settle for the first person who shows any level of interest.

However, the uncomfortable truth is that having a child with the wrong person is even worse than marrying the wrong person. Why? Because you'll be tied to that person for the rest of your life due to sharing a child together. That's why it's even more important to be extremely selective about who you choose to have in your life and father your children.

If I could have one wish, it would be for you to never rush into a relationship without considering your own worth. Love yourself so deeply that you refuse to settle for anything less than the very best.

CHAPTER 43

"Part 1 ~ Mother or lover?"

*O*kay, so you meet a guy you really like. He ticks all your boxes and is definitely your type on paper. You see a future with him more than you have with any other guy in a very long time, and you're excited. But, my darling, I have something very important that I need to tell you.

If you want to maintain this guy's attraction, then you really need to listen to this: there is one sure-fire way to lose a guy's attraction to you... mothering him!

There is a huge difference between mothering and nurturing. Read that again!

As women, we often have an innate nurturing nature that makes it easy for us to act like a mother hen, fussing around and trying to help and do everything for him. While it's nice to do this for our children, we shouldn't be doing it for our adult partners!

"What do you mean by 'mothering'?"

Well, when it comes to mothering a grown man, some well-meaning behaviours can sometimes go overboard. These include doing things for him that he is perfectly capable of doing himself, such as:

1. If he's forgetful, you are constantly reminding him of basic information like a doctor's appointment or to book his MOT.

2. Taking charge of tasks that you think he can't handle, like washing up or cooking dinner.

3. Correcting and guiding him, treating him as if he's not capable, and scolding him like he is a child if he gets it wrong.

While it may come from a place of love or concern, it's important to remember that grown men are quite capable on their own. The more you do everything for him, the less effort he'll put in himself. It can be overwhelming when you're left with an endless to-do list, and it's easy to start feeling less attracted to him because you might see him as someone who can't take care of himself.

Treating your partner like you're his mother can have a seriously negative impact on your relationship. It may make him feel insecure and suffocated when you're around. Men value feeling respected, useful, and masculine, so this kind of treatment can quickly dampen the passion between you and even lead to resentment or rebellion from your partner. It's like how children assert themselves by breaking away from their parents.

Men fall in love with a woman they are attracted to … But this is the kicker: He stays in love with the woman who makes him feel wanted and makes him want to be the best version of himself. Moreover, if he constantly feels inadequate around you, his self-esteem will likely suffer, and he may not show you as much love anymore.

"So, how do I distinguish between mothering and nurturing?"

Ahhh, well, here are some examples…

Example of nurturing:

When he comes to your house, you can ask, "Would you like a drink? What can I get you? Would you like a bit of lime in it? How about a sandwich? Are you feeling hungry?"

Example of mothering:

When he comes to your house, you can ask, "Would you like a drink? Oh, you prefer beer? Do you think that's a good idea, considering you've already had alcohol twice this week? How about a nice, cold glass of water instead? Did you take your vitamins? Are you sure you want another sandwich? I think you might have already eaten too much wheat today!"

A guy may enjoy being taken care of all day long, but trust me, it can diminish his sexual attraction towards you very quickly! It can also be difficult to recover from once you start down this path.

If you want to stop treating a man like your child, here's what you can do: First, refrain from doing things for him that he is perfectly capable of doing himself. When he asks you where his keys are, simply say, "I don't know," and let him find them on his own. Additionally, it's best to avoid giving fashion advice; a grown man should know how to dress himself without your input. Lastly, resist the urge to tidy up after him if he leaves his clothes lying around. It's important to show love, care, and support, but it's time to stop playing the role of his mother.

Now, it is crucial to view your partner as someone who is capable and reliable. Instead of constantly reminding him about things he should already be aware of, give him the space to handle things on his own.

Don't become his personal calendar – let him take charge of his responsibilities. Just assume he is a responsible adult who can handle his own stuff. If he keeps forgetting appointments or events, he'll eventually get better at managing his schedule. Also, try not to talk down to your partner as if he is a little kid; nobody likes being scolded for no reason, especially a man!

It's also important to take the time to discuss responsibilities and expectations. Let him know what you expect, but avoid micromanaging every little mistake. Trust that things will work out, even if they don't go exactly as planned. And remember, it's crucial for both of you to learn how to tackle challenges independently, so resist the urge to constantly swoop in and save the day.

If you start feeling like you're his mother, it can kill the attraction you have for him. And it works the other way around, too. If he starts seeing you as a mother figure, things can go downhill FAST! It's hard to come back from a loss of attraction. Men appreciate being taken care of, BUT never forget that acting like their mother is not exactly a turn-on. You want to keep that sexual attraction alive and kicking, so it is important to also set boundaries. On that note …

"Part 2 ~ Boundaries"

As independent adults, we are solely responsible for our own physical, emotional, social, and financial well-being.

- Maintaining physical health.
- Sticking to routines.
- Staying in touch with friends and family.
- Taking financial responsibility for purchases.

If you frequently find yourself taking on responsibility for your partner's relationships, wellness, finances, or other areas, it's important to ask yourself:

- Why am I doing this?
- What is my motive here?

- Do I hope that my partner will feel dependent on me so they never leave?
- Am I trying to protect my partner from facing the consequences of their actions?
- Am I trying to make up for my partner's deficits?
- Do my partner's deficits leave me feeling uncomfortable

"Why is it bad to help my man avoid the negative consequences of his own choices?"

Well, this is a little realised fact … you know, when we try to soften the impact of other people's poor choices, we're preventing them from learning valuable lessons. Have you ever found yourself downplaying the consequences when your partner has a meltdown, perhaps due to a poor decision or losing his temper? You might think you're helping him, but you're enabling his bad behaviour. If he doesn't have to face the consequences, why would he feel motivated to change?

We also help our partners avoid negative consequences by not expressing justified anger, sadness, or discomfort with their actions. When we withhold our feelings out of fear of hurting his feelings, we are simply managing his emotions, which is NOT our responsibility. When setting a boundary, there's no need to smooth over the tension or protect him from feeling uncomfortable. It's natural for people to feel bad and weird when they have crossed a line.

"What exactly are boundaries?"

Boundaries serve as our way of defining what is acceptable and what is not. Their purpose is not to control others but to safeguard ourselves and preserve our authenticity. However, for a boundary to truly be effective, we must consistently uphold it, even when it is crossed. Otherwise, they become mere words without any meaningful action to back them up.

Imagine, for instance, you tell your partner, "If you don't stop being mean to me, I'm leaving." If they continue to mistreat you, then you must be prepared to leave. Otherwise, your so-called "boundary" was nothing more than a deceptive attempt to change them under false pretences.

"But what if my partner has no desire to change?"

Change is something that originates from within. While we can support or hinder others in their healing journeys, we can lead a horse to water; we cannot make it drink.

Healing requires an individual's willingness. For instance, if someone is not ready to overcome an addiction, we cannot educate them to do so. If someone is not prepared to confront their trauma, we cannot force them to heal. And if someone is burdened by the weight of their past, we cannot forcibly remove that baggage from them.

When our partner is unable or unwilling to provide us with the closeness we desire, we may start behaving in ways that seek their attention. This is our attempt to elicit a reaction from them, even if it's only for a brief moment, in order to re-establish that bond. We might resort to tactics such as giving them silent treatment, withholding intimacy, trying to provoke jealousy, or even threatening to end the relationship (does this sound familiar?).

We engage in this behaviour not because we want to end things, sever ties, or pursue someone new but rather because we desire a change in how our partner treats us. We believe that these tantrums could potentially be the catalyst for bringing about that desired change. We think that if we threaten them, they will just miraculously start to treat us right.

When I was younger, I used emotional outbursts as a means of seeking attention from my partner when he wasn't willingly giving it. Instead of recognising that we both had a responsibility to meet our own needs at that time, he needed space, and I needed to self-soothe. I unintentionally created a dynamic where he felt obligated to prioritise MY needs over his own.

Needless to say, it never ended well, and I was completely unaware of my behaviour at the time. Now, as I work with my clients, I observe many of them engaging in similar patterns within their relationships. And, if I'm honest, I look back at when I was like that and cringe. I wasn't even aware at the time that I was doing it. I just knew I wanted a particular outcome and acted out to get what I wanted.

If you have consciously or unconsciously used the tactics mentioned above, you're not alone. Many of us have had to let go of our toxic illusions of control. As we move forward, it's important to understand what actually falls within our sphere of control and learn to live within those boundaries.

"But how can I prevent myself from doing this?"

At first, the idea of letting go of control can be terrifying. Control may have been our way of managing the world and creating a sense of safety for ourselves. But imagine a life where the only person you have to control is yourself. A life where you let others do what is right for them while you focus on making the right choices for yourself. Well, I'm here to tell you that it is possible!

Remember, it's always wise to ask for permission before offering your help and to accept their answer without questioning it. Help is most appreciated when it is given freely, without any hidden motives. So, it's important to start by asking, "Do you need help?" If they decline your offer, respect their decision. Avoid the temptation to ask, "Are you sure?" Remember, you can only help yourself.

To break the cycle of excessive control, it is crucial to take a vital step: learning to self-soothe and take responsibility for your own emotional state.

If you find yourself feeling distressed, then here are some tips on what you can do:

- When you feel on the verge of a powerful emotional reaction, allow yourself to sit quietly with the feeling and process it.
- When a strong emotion arises in the presence of others, make sure to take a few minutes or more to be completely alone. If you need even more space, such as a night to yourself, then allow yourself to take it.
- If you need support, have a shortlist of trusted friends and family members or a coach whom you can rely on.

These techniques will not only reduce your reliance on your partner but also instil in you a deep sense of resilience. Instead of feeling like a victim amidst an emotional storm, you need to become aware of the internal resources you possess to weather the turbulence.

"What happens if my partner is unwilling to work on an issue?"

As I have already mentioned, when someone shows you who they are, believe them! If I had accepted my ex-partner's statement that he was unwilling to work on our relationship, I would have saved myself nine long months of futilely trying to change his mind. It would have also spared me two months of sleepless nights and heartache.

I have realised (the hard way) that resolving relationship problems requires effort from both parties. Both individuals must take responsibility for their role and actively work towards making positive changes. If someone is unwilling to change, they will likely remain stuck in their old habits. Therefore, it is essential to consider whether you can genuinely find contentment with someone who refuses to change.

Remember: You cannot heal someone else's wounds or carry their baggage. Your efforts cannot transform an emotionally unavailable person into an emotionally available one. It has been helpful for me to create a list of non-negotiables that serve as a guide when deciding if a relationship is healthy enough for me to maintain. My non-negotiables include qualities and behaviours that must or must not be present in my partner. These include:

- *Absolutely no physical or mental abuse,*
- *No substance addiction.*

- *No form of coercion.*
- Additionally,
- *I greatly appreciate the ability to navigate through tough times together and communicate any issues calmly.*
- *He must have a good sense of humour.*
- *He must be kind.*

Side note: There is no point in having non-negotiables that can be negotiated!

While it's tempting to hope that our partners can magically understand our needs, the reality is that they can't read our minds, no matter how much they love us. We need to verbally communicate our boundaries clearly from the start and give them a fair opportunity to respond appropriately. If we don't do this, we might find ourselves resorting to old habits of manipulation to get what we want.

Boundaries are like personal body armour. They serve to keep the negative things out and safeguard our inner peace. Whether it's about physical touch, time management, protecting our belongings, or even setting communication limits – boundaries empower us to maintain control.

Not sure where you might need to set a boundary? Consider when and where you feel resentful.

Once you've identified your resentment, you can set a boundary with the person involved. For those of us who are new to expressing our needs directly, finding the right words can often be the most challenging part.

At first, it might feel like a heavy burden. You may even get a sense of power from controlling others. So, the idea of taking responsibility for yourself may seem seemed overwhelming. But let me tell you, it made a huge difference and helped me tremendously.

CHAPTER

44

"How do you know?"

*A*lright, imagine you've found yourself a great guy and things are going well. But let's be honest, how can you know if he's the one for you? Time may pass, whether it's a few days, months, or even years, but the important question remains: how do you determine if he's truly worth your ongoing investment of time, effort, and love?

In earlier chapters, we discussed the importance of having standards and not wasting time on someone who doesn't meet them. By sticking to this approach, you can easily identify and weed out those who aren't a good fit for you. Typically, this process of sussing out happens within the first few weeks of getting to know them.

Dating can be tough, especially when you're longing for a relationship. It's tempting to settle for anyone just because you crave that romantic connection, especially when there's no one else in the picture at the moment. But remember, it's important to prioritise your inner happiness and not let desperation cloud your judgment, even in the early stages. Keep your standards high!

No matter what you're going through, the right person for you will not judge or look down on you. You'll feel comfortable opening up to him about anything, including embarrassing moments or moments when you weren't proud of yourself, and he won't criticise you for it. He'll be there for you and do anything he can to help you in those situations.

I asked you to reflect on past relationships that didn't work out, and if you're being honest with yourself, you will notice that there were red flags from the start that you overlooked.

As a rule, we choose to ignore these warning signs because, deep down, we desperately want to believe that we have found our perfect match. We love the chemistry and the great sex, and we love how he holds our hand or pays for dinner. So, we ignore how angry and screaming he becomes when another car cuts him off on the road, how he can't hold down a job, how he doesn't want kids, but you do, or how rude he is to his mother. ...Remember that people are always showing us who they are, and we need to learn to believe them and accept them for who they are or move on.

When I look back on my first serious relationship, I have to admit that I saw the warning signals like big flashing beacons right from the beginning, but I chose to completely ignore them. I disregarded significant red flags, even though they were obvious, because, to be honest, I was desperate for a relationship. All my friends were in relationships, and I was feeling lonely. We would argue about various issues, and he would promise to change, and he did... for two weeks! Then, we would just fall back into the same old issues all over again.

To be brutally honest, deep down, I was afraid that no one else would want me the way he did. Despite knowing he wasn't the right one for me, as he tended to become mean and unpredictably aggressive when upset, I tolerated it and made excuses because I didn't want to be alone or go through the process of getting to know someone new. Unfortunately, I paid a steep price later for ignoring all the warning signs. That relationship ultimately brought me to my knees. It ended in court battles and police involvement, but that's a whole other story!

Sometimes, we may doubt ourselves when the signs are brief or subtle. But if something starts to bother us or we notice any signs of jealousy, anger, aggression, spitefulness, meanness, or anything else that raises a red flag, it's important to trust our gut instincts. If we're not careful, we might end up wasting our time and energy on someone who doesn't deserve our love, support, attention, or loyalty in the long run. It's important to be wise about where we invest our time, love and energy. I had a good friend who always used to say, "The way a relationship begins is often the way it ends," and now I know she could be right!

Relationships, as you probably already know, are always a bit unpredictable. No matter how hard we try, we can never guarantee how things will turn out. But you know what? That's part of the excitement! The unknown is what keeps the fire alive and makes love so thrilling. Nobody knows what the future holds. That's just a fact of life.

"But how will I know if he is 'The One'?"

Oh, you know your partner is the right one to marry when you love him and are willing to make sacrifices for his happiness, and in return, he is willing to make sacrifices for your happiness.

I need to pass on this golden nugget of wisdom to you. People often overlook the practical aspects of a relationship, but they are SO incredibly important. Falling in love is the easy bit, but after several years of witnessing someone's annoying traits, you tend to become more inclined to choose to continue loving them when you've already worked through the practical stuff, such as:

1. Finances: How do you see money? Are you good at saving money? What are your financial goals, expectations, and habits? How do you feel about debt? How much debt do each of you currently have? It's important to have these discussions and

be on the same page, as finances can be a major source of stress in a relationship.

2. Parenting: Deciding whether to have children, determining the desired number of children, timing and when to start a family, views on the division of parenting responsibilities, and approaches to discipline and guiding children's behaviour are all crucial aspects to discuss. These discussions shape the future of a family and the parenting journey.

3. When it comes to domestic duties and cleanliness standards, it is important to evaluate the level of cleanliness that both you and your partner can tolerate. If you already feel that your share of responsibilities is disproportionately high, be aware that this burden may increase significantly when children are involved. Typically, these circumstances do not improve but rather worsen over time.

4. Religion and politics. Could you be happy with your partner who has different beliefs from yours? You don't need to see eye to eye on everything, but it's crucial to value each other's perspectives and reasoning.

5. Extended family expectations. How tight-knit are you with your family? And what about your other half and his lot?

6. Careers. How important is your career to you? What about your partner's career? If one of you needs to move for a major promotion or opportunity, who will be willing to make the sacrifice? Is one of you interested in being a stay-at-home parent? How do you each feel about that?

7. Sex. Partners need to have similar sex drives. If one person constantly feels pressured for sex while the other consistently feels sexually frustrated, it can negatively impact the relationship. It is crucial to be on the same page regarding sexual

desires right from the beginning. Open and candid discussions about sex should be encouraged without any feelings of embarrassment or shame.

8. Communication. Does your partner make you feel good about yourself? Do you share a sense of humour or at least respect each other's senses of humour? Do you handle problems as a 2-man team? Does he fight fair? Are arguments productive? Does he listen to your side and genuinely consider what you say, or is he focused on "winning" every argument? Communication problems can magnify the original issue. If you don't communicate well and kindly, it can create a divide in your relationship.

You know what's funny? When we're getting to know someone, we sometimes get fixated on one good thing they have going for them. But we often overlook other things that are just as important to us. It's easy to get caught up in one positive aspect and start imagining that they have all these other qualities, too.

A close friend of mine began dating a guy with an incredible ambition for his career, which she found highly attractive. She admired his passion for building his brand and his future aspirations. However, as they spent more time together, she began to realise that he rarely made time to see her and that his business always took precedence. Because of his ambition, he constantly worked and neglected their relationship. Even during their dates, he would interrupt conversations to answer work calls or reply to emails. Unfortunately, he didn't value their relationship enough.

Consequently, she felt unloved and neglected, which ultimately led to their breakup. It's a shame because she genuinely admired his strong work ethic and dedication.

However, without that emotional connection, they simply couldn't make it work.

In the end, both you and your spouse are bound to grow and evolve. However, if you start with shared values and keep communication open, you significantly increase the likelihood of growing together in the right direction. Couples who have been married for 60 years and still hold hands in the park at the age of 85 are a testament to the strength of walking side by side throughout their lives. If you don't start on the same path initially, can you imagine how challenging it will be to stay on that path as time goes on?

CHAPTER

45

"Keeping that flame alive".

$\mathcal{I}$n this book, you'll have discovered a wealth of advice on captivating men. However, it wouldn't be complete without sharing tips on maintaining that spark over time and being mindful of potential deal-breakers. You may have heard the saying "opposites attract." We've all witnessed couples where one is extroverted, and the other introverted, or one is boisterous while the other prefers silence. Nevertheless, it's crucial to recognise that personality traits differ from values.

We all know those people who love to talk a big game about their ambitions and dreams but don't actually take any action to pursue them. They seem happy staying in their comfort zone and show no willingness to put in the necessary effort to achieve what they claim to want. Instead of taking responsibility for their lack of success, they often blame external factors and ignore their own lack of progress. Wishing for ambition and working towards your dreams is one thing, but actually living it is a whole different story.

Here's why this concept is important for our happiness going forward: No matter how much we talk about our core values with someone, it's all just empty words unless we see them living by those values. They may agree with us on what's important, but actions speak louder than words. When choosing a partner, it's important to base our decisions on their current standards rather than just their potential. Instead of getting caught up in what someone could be, let's put our energy into appreciating the person standing right in front of us.

It's not just about his values but also about his standards. Each person's values have their own level of importance and intensity. Just because two people enjoy adventure doesn't mean they have the exact same idea of what it means to be adventurous. Adventure means something different to each person. While some people dream of conquering Mount Everest, others consider themselves adventurous simply by trying a new dish at a fancy seafood restaurant.

So, instead of trying to shape others into who we want them to be, let's make sure they have the value that we need from the start and appreciate them for who they are right now … but also ask yourself if you are happy with who they are now. Can people grow and change? Absolutely! But it's important not to rely solely on someone else's transformation for our personal happiness. It's wiser to focus on our own journey and not place too much expectation on influencing someone else's path.

From the moment we start talking to someone, it's crucial to keep our eyes WIDE OPEN and take off the rose-tinted glasses. Are they truly demonstrating, through their ACTIONS and not just words, that they share the same values as us? This is something worth paying attention to, especially if we're attracted to them. When we spend time with them, do we witness them living up to the same values that we hold dear in our own lives? Talk is cheap, so don't rely solely on what they say, but rather on what they do!

"But how do I find a guy who ticks all the boxes on my list?"

Look, I'm not saying he has to live his life exactly like you or share all of your opinions and life goals. The odds of meeting someone who does are probably lower than England winning the World Cup!

We all have our unique ways of expressing our values and making life decisions. When it comes to generosity, everyone has their own way of showing it. Some people express their generosity by being extra caring and considerate towards their loved ones and best friends. Others choose to regularly get involved in charity work to help those who are less fortunate or buy big-ticket presents. And for some, it's as simple as picking up the bill after a meal out.

Here's some valuable advice for you: never enter a relationship expecting a guy to change his deal-breaker qualities for you. It's important to be realistic and find someone who already meets your non-negotiables. Trust me, if a guy claims he'll change, you'll likely find yourself fighting an uphill battle.

In my honest opinion, two crucial values hold significant importance in a relationship:

Honesty and *Teamwork.*

If both parties possess and exhibit these values, there is potential to overcome differences and make things work. If travelling is important to you but your partner is a homebody, it's unlikely that they will suddenly change their mindset. If you're a neat freak and he lives like Steptoe, it's an issue that will always make you miserable. Sure, at the beginning, he might make some adjustments to his behaviour to prevent losing you. But let's be real; true and long-lasting change goes beyond that. It demands genuine determination, unwavering commitment, and a sincere belief in personal growth, regardless of whether he's in a relationship with you.

If your guy doesn't have the drive to better himself for his own sake, then don't hold your breath, expecting him to suddenly transform into a better man just for you. It's best to manage your expectations and focus on finding someone who is genuinely motivated to grow and improve. Teamwork is equally important as the first value. It motivates him to share his efforts to enhance your relationship and bring you happiness. When it comes to teamwork, it's about his belief in your ability to overcome any relationship issues by working together. Remember, actions speak louder than words. If you want to know if a man truly values these principles, observe what he does.

So, when you open up to him about what brings you joy, does he listen and make an effort to meet those needs? Or does he get defensive and ignore your desires just to protect his ego? When you're in a tight spot, does he have your back, or does he disappear? He doesn't need to know exactly how to keep you content, but it does matter that he genuinely makes an effort and puts in the work.

Being a team means having the power to guide someone in the right direction. But here's the thing: he must genuinely want to make you happy for it to work. You can support them in changing their approach and overcoming obstacles together but remember that you can't force someone to have good intentions or certain values – that must come from within them.

If you and a new partner share similar values and standards, your dedication to growing as a team and working together is more likely to result in a successful relationship. Both of you must align on what truly matters to you. If you meet a guy with completely different values, don't waste your time trying to transform him into something he probably won't become.

Here's my honest take on why relationships can sometimes go downhill:

When you start dating someone with whom you have intense sexual chemistry and quickly jump into bed, your body releases a mix of chemicals that can make you feel euphoric and on cloud nine. You just want to turn into molten larvae and melt into him. These chemicals also create intense cravings, making you want to be with them constantly, staying up late into the night, chatting away, and getting busy in the bedroom while ignoring any red flags.

But here's the reality check: after a while, things start to shift and change. The initial surge of chemicals in our bodies gives way to a more consistent flow. The intense buzz of staying up all night and being unable to resist their company, as well as the passionate sex, eventually subsides. This is when you get to see the real person in front of you, what you have in common, and who they are.

If he is a keeper, and you want to keep him hooked, you've got to bring the excitement, captivate his attention, and throw in a few surprises here and there. That's how you keep things interesting and fun. But hey, if what you need is someone who will truly listen to you without talking back, create a safe space for expression, help tackle your problems head-on, see things solely from your point of view, and go the extra mile to make you happy, then my friend, it's time to book an appointment with a therapist!

Relationships are never quite as we imagine them to be. People are far more complex than we often give them credit for. They are like jigsaw puzzles with many odd-shaped pieces, and it takes time to understand them fully. Building a deep connection with someone requires genuine love, attention, and a good sense of humour. These qualities are priceless and go beyond any material possessions. The beauty of relationships is that when you give these gifts wholeheartedly, you raise your chances of receiving so much more in return. You gain trust, understanding, and an emotional bond that can't be measured by anything tangible. It's amazing how the act of giving can enrich your life in ways you never expected.

Continuing to be generous with your love, attention, and sense of fun is crucial in forming a deeper connection with your dream guy. By showing him genuine affection and making him feel valued, you are laying a strong foundation for your relationship. It's important to keep in mind that relationships require effort and nurturing. While there may be moments when you feel like you're making sacrifices or facing challenges, the rewards of a deeper connection will far outweigh any perceived losses along the way.

Investing time and energy into building a meaningful bond will result in more fulfilling experiences and a stronger emotional connection with your partner. Remember to cherish the journey of forming this connection. Focus on finding joy in the little moments shared, whether it's through heartfelt conversations or fun activities that bring both of you closer. Embrace each step of the process as an opportunity for growth and discovery.

By maintaining an open heart, being attentive, and fostering a sense of playfulness within your relationship, you can create a loving environment where both you and your dream guy can thrive. So, keep spreading love generously and fearlessly, and do not be scared. Remember that even if things don't work out with one particular guy, you are strong and independent … you will be just fine!

CHAPTER
46

"Conclusion"

Dear reader

Love is an incredible source of internal happiness. Hopefully, this book has empowered you to take control of your romantic journey and equipped you with the knowledge to navigate the realm of love and understand men better.

However, it's crucial to remember that while love is significant, life encompasses much more. Countless other aspects bring joy and fulfilment, such as personal growth, meaningful relationships with family and friends, pursuing passions and interests, and simply enjoying life's little pleasures. So, keep an open heart for love, but never forget to embrace all the other beautiful experiences life offers!

No matter how your personal story unfolds, the advice shared in this book aims to help you achieve the life and love you have always dreamed of. While the insights primarily focus on finding and keeping the right partner, they ultimately revolve around working on yourself, embracing self-love and inner self-belief, and building a meaningful and satisfying life that brings you true joy and happiness.

This game of life offers no guarantees, and tomorrow is not promised. We may experience the joys of love and intense attraction, only to have them disappear just as quickly. But here's the key: no matter what challenges life throws at you, remember that you have the inner strength to handle them and come out of the storm perfectly intact. Settling for any old relationship won't bring you happiness, and you deserve nothing but happiness in your life!

Just remember to stay true to yourself and believe in what you stand for. By the way, I think you are bloody amazing! Never forget that you are in charge of your destiny, and your decisions will impact your future. Make sure they are good decisions. We all live the life we choose, so embrace who you are, and I guarantee you'll feel more confident and see some serious positive changes in all areas of your life!

You can truly empower your life by embracing the art of creating instead of waiting, operating from a mindset of abundance rather than scarcity, developing and adhering to the attributes of a person with high self-esteem, practising self-love, upholding your standards and boundaries, and understanding that YOU are in control of your own choices.

Developing these skills will enhance your self-worth and positively impact every aspect of your life. It's a lifelong journey. Not only will your love life improve, but your mood, attitude, job performance, friendships, and ability to set and achieve personal goals will also improve.

Simply put, the main message here is to believe in yourself. By doing so, you will be able to take advantage of incredible opportunities and live an incredible life, my darling.

However, I regret that I cannot do all the work for you. It is now your responsibility to take charge and steer your ship. This is your chance to seize the opportunity, and always remember to BE THE PRIZE!

Go get 'em, girl!
Kel x

I can sense your excitement! I'm eager to hear all the juicy details. Please keep me updated and share how everything unfolds at www.kelscoaching.com.
Looking forward to hearing from you!

Printed in Great Britain
by Amazon

41773045R00199